A

Jim Richardson has re
show winning perfection
years. His work is featu
Classic Car, Classic
Australian Classic Car n
vious books, and his res
Video Magazine, airing
divide their time betwee
New Zealand.

AC

I want to thank the foll
many photos in this bo
John Sloane for their w
great deal of gratitude to
welding and who has sp
in order to make this boo
her valuable insight and
wife, Bette, for her creati

RDSON

Do-It-Yourself Guide to
ENGINE & CHASSIS
DETAILING

BY JIM RICHARDSON

OVERSEAS DISTRIBUTION BY:

BROOKLANDS BOOKS LTD.
P.O. BOX 146, Cobham, Surrey, KT11 1LG, England
Telephone 01932 865051 • FAX 01932 868803

BROOKLANDS BOOKS LTD.
1/81 Darley Street, P.O. Box 199, Mona Vale, NSW 2103, Australia
Telephone 2 999 78428 • FAX 2 997 95799

PRODUCTION BY
TAMARA BAECHTEL

COPY EDITED BY
MONICA DWYER ABRES

ISBN 1-884089-46-1
PART No. SA62

CARTECH, INC., 11605 KOST DAM RD., NORTH BRANCH, MN 55056

CONTENTS

Engine & Chassis DETAILING
Setting Up Shop

When a '46 Chrysler, a '56 Chevrolet, and a '66 Mustang have been put right — by that I mean exactly the way they came from the factory — such cars are a pleasure to drive. They make you realize how good cars actually were, even many years ago. Unfortunately, most classic cars seen today, though they are restored cosmetically and their engines are rebuilt, have marginal brakes, sloppy steering, and dead springs. For some reason, these less glamorous items get short shrift in the restoration process.

I believe it has something to do with the facts that fresh, clean, sparkling engines and flawless paint jobs bring oohs and ahs at get-togethers. In contrast, a good brake system, tight steering, and a freshly rebuilt and carefully detailed suspension and chassis go comparatively unnoticed. That is, of course, unless you drive the car. Marginal brakes, sagging springs, leaking shock absorbers,

and sloppy steering make the car hard to turn, hard to stop, and miserable as a means of transport. Neglected long enough, these components will make your classic a danger to yourself and others.

I also believe that many of the less glamorous components in a classic are not understood as well as the engines, transmissions, and paintwork. They are neglected not so much from carelessness, but from ignorance. We have forgotten how well Dad's '57 DeSoto handled and stopped when new, so we believe everything is fine, that these cars just weren't as enjoyable to drive then as the modern ones are now.

Nothing could be further from the truth. Such cars could loaf along the then-new interstate highways at 80 mph, floating on soft, balanced, well-tuned suspensions. They were massive machines, yet they steered effortlessly and stopped well, considering their size and their drum brakes. So

how do you make an old car's chassis right again?

That's what this book is about. First we'll talk about the skills and tools that will serve you in your efforts, as well as how to avoid the pitfalls common to car restoration. Then we'll tell you how to troubleshoot, disassemble, and rebuild the basic components of your car's chassis and how to detail these components so that they will look good and work well for years to come.

Of course, many more modern cars don't have conventional frames, but they do have integrated, welded-in braces and channels that need to be rust free and healthy if the car is going to be safe. For that reason there are chapters on rust busting and patch welding that will tell you how to put a unit-bodied car right and how to keep it that way.

If you drive your classic, you'll definitely want to make sure the chassis components are as fresh

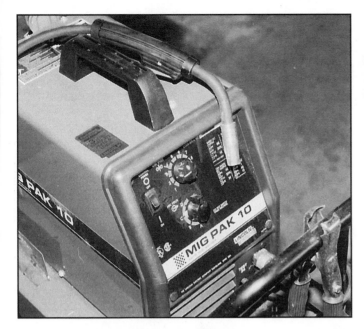

A welder such as this Lincoln MIG Pak 10 for home use is not absolutely necessary. But without one you will have to farm out any welding, which could easily exceed the cost of this easy-to-use home unit.

A blast cabinet, such as this Eastwood benchtop unit, can save hours of scraping and grinding.

as the rest of the car, because nothing else you do can make such a profound difference in the enjoyment of your vehicle. Fortunately, none of the systems associated with the chassis are particularly difficult or complex to work on, and few special tools are required. There are some basic requirements, though, and we'll tell you what they are here. Shall we get started?

SETTING UP SHOP

You've decided to do it — you're going to take a classic car apart and put it together again, making it new or better than new in the process. It's a big undertaking, but thousands have done it before you, so if you can learn from their experiences — and their mistakes — you won't have much trouble. But first things first. You'll need a place to work and the proper tools to do the job.

FACILITIES

To begin with, a two-car garage that you can dedicate to your project for some months, perhaps years, is a must. Don't even consider doing the job in your drive-

way, though there are plenty of tasks that can be performed outdoors. The reason you need at least a two-car garage is because you will want to store car parts in an orderly fashion, protecting them from curious pets, children, and the elements. You will also need to protect your tools from theft; quite a few implements will be accumulated before the job is done.

THE BOTTOM LINE

There are certain basic hand tools you can't do without, such as a good socket set with a 1/2-in. drive, a set of open-end, box, and combination wrenches, a vise, a mechanic's creeper, and an engine stand. Other, more specialized tools such as a torque wrench, circlip pliers, and electrical pliers can be picked up as they are needed. Also, check with local rental yards to see which tools, such as hoists and drum pullers, are available. Then there are tools that make chassis and engine-room restoration much easier. You will want to purchase them as soon as possible.

ABOVE THE BOTTOM LINE

Some examples of helpful tools for restoration are a MIG welder or a stick welder; a high-volume, low-pressure (HVLP) painting rig; a fairly large media-blasting cabinet; a high-speed grinder-buffer; an air compressor; and a parts-washing bin. Money spent on these items (as little as $1,500 at this writing) will save you thousands of dollars and as many hours in the long run, making the results of your efforts much more professional.

Another tool that I now consider necessary is a powder-coating gun. Powder coating is many times more durable than paint and easier to apply. I wouldn't do a chassis or an engine without one these days. The device retails for about $150 and will pay for itself in short order.

LIGHTING

Good lighting is required. Pick up half a dozen inexpensive fluorescent light fixtures at a home-improvement store and install them. Light is especially important for painting and it will make assembly and disassembly much easier. Mount the light according

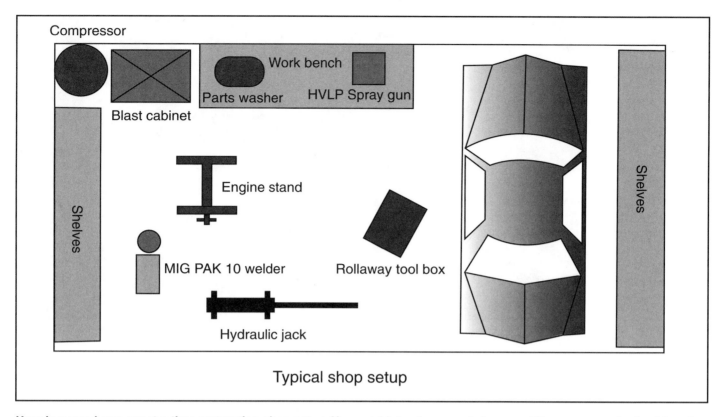

Compressor

Blast cabinet

Parts washer

Work bench

HVLP Spray gun

Engine stand

Shelves

MIG PAK 10 welder

Rollaway tool box

Hydraulic jack

Shelves

Typical shop setup

Here is a good one-car-at-a-time restoration-shop setup. You need lots of room, shelves, and the necessary tools at hand.

to local codes to minimize the possibility of sparks or arcing when you are shooting paint.

SAFETY

If your garage has a water heater with a pilot light, consider moving it outdoors to its own metal shed, or at least walling it off and venting it to the outside. You will be dealing with a number of volatile liquids, including gasoline, when you restore your car's fuel system. A flame can cause fumes to flash, with disastrous results.

A heavy-duty fire extinguisher is a must. A large exhaust fan and plenty of ventilation are important, too. You will also need a respirator mask with fresh charcoal filters for painting, as well as heavy cotton or leather work gloves. Safety glasses or goggles are a must, too, as is a first-aid kit. Beating up your knuckles is a byproduct of the job. I would also recommend that you have a telephone installed or take a remote or cell phone to the garage with you whenever you work on your car.

SHELVES

You will also want to build or buy some shelving. A typical older car has as many as 5,500 parts, so storing things in an orderly fashion is critical to the project. Inexpensive metal shelves from a discount hardware store are fine, providing you secure them to the walls. Drawers are nice to have, too. I found a sturdy old chest of drawers at a secondhand store in which to keep delicate or fragile tools such as my voltmeter, timing light, machine tools, and other devices.

BENCH

A large, sturdy workbench is also important. Buy or build one that is high enough so you don't have to slump to work at it. You will be putting in hours on items such as brake cylinders, carburetors, fuel pumps, and steering units, and you will want to lay them out in systematic order. Finally, if you can afford a rollaway, buy one. You'll be glad you did. Having tools handy will speed the job tremendously and make it much more enjoyable.

COMPRESSOR

A compressor also is necessary. A large one is no longer indispensable for shooting paint because the new HVLP spray units are either turbine powered or require a more modest source of compressed air. But you will need at least a two-horsepower compressor (five horses would be better) that puts out seven cubic feet of air per minute at 80 psi for your blasting cabinet. You also will need an air source for tools such as a powder-coating gun, sanders, and grinders.

JACK

Get a good, heavy-duty jack. Don't even think of trying to use a bumper jack or the jack that came with the car. They can let you down at the worst time, damaging your car and causing you injury. A large, hydraulic jack that can easily support the front of your car is what you want, and they are not as expensive as you may think. And don't forget sturdy jack stands. Never work on a car

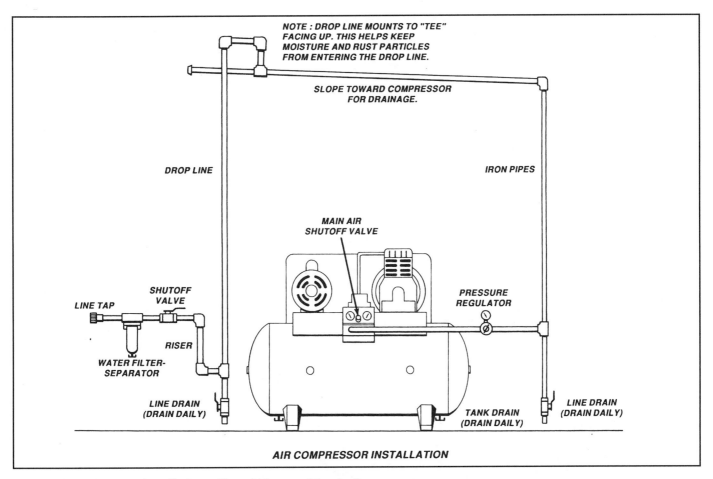

NOTE : DROP LINE MOUNTS TO "TEE" FACING UP. THIS HELPS KEEP MOISTURE AND RUST PARTICLES FROM ENTERING THE DROP LINE.

SLOPE TOWARD COMPRESSOR FOR DRAINAGE.

DROP LINE

IRON PIPES

MAIN AIR SHUTOFF VALVE

PRESSURE REGULATOR

SHUTOFF VALVE

LINE TAP

RISER

WATER FILTER-SEPARATOR

LINE DRAIN (DRAIN DAILY)

TANK DRAIN (DRAIN DAILY)

LINE DRAIN (DRAIN DAILY)

AIR COMPRESSOR INSTALLATION

Proper air compressor installation will avoid hours of frustration.

while it is resting on a jack. Doing so can be a deadly mistake.

You won't need everything at once. Start with the hand tools and less expensive items, then buy the bigger items as you need them. One other thing I've found to be indispensable over the years is the Eastwood catalog. I keep one at home and one in my shop at all times. Frequently, the special tool that makes a difficult task easy is just a phone call away.

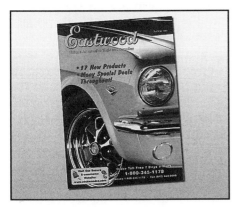

Just call 1-800-345-1178 for a free catalog. This catalog has tools for every phase of restoration.

Racing Dollies are handy for moving the car around the shop.

Engine & Chassis DETAILING
Media Blasting

It's the quickest way to rid parts of rust, paint, and scale.

It took me a couple of restorations to wise up. I spent hundreds of hours scraping, grinding, and brushing rust and scale off old parts and accessories before I acquired a media-blasting cabinet. A cabinet makes an otherwise dirty, lengthy task quick and easy. Granted, cabinets cost between $300 and $800, but in the end they are less expensive than taking everything to a professional sandblaster. Depending on how you value your time, your own cabinet can save you even more.

Another advantage is that you will know the job was done right, using the correct medium. Regular sand, or, alternatively, silicone carbide in the wrong hands with lots of pressure behind it, can ruin just about anything. Sand or silicone carbide are okay for heavy castings, although they can leave very pitted surfaces. For most purposes you will want to use aluminum oxide or glass beads.

GETTING IT TOGETHER

My son and I ordered our blasting cabinet through the mail. It came in several flat boxes ready for assembly. The job took about five hours and required a pop-rivet gun. (Actually two, because the first one we bought was a cheapy and it came apart about halfway through the job. After that we headed for the local tool store and purchased the fancy, $20 model.)

The cabinet we purchased came from the Eastwood Company and was complete. All we had to add at the end was a shop vacuum, the compressor hose, and a water trap. The stand bolts together, then the big sheet metal box and hopper are pop-riveted together. We found that welder's reach-around clamps were great for holding the panels in alignment while riveting.

Once the box and hopper were together, we sealed the seams and rivets with a tube of silicone that was included in the kit. Don't skip this step because you don't want to breathe the

dust and particles from the blasting media. It can be vicious, sharp stuff. Large doors at either end of the cabinet are sealed with soft rubber and make loading easy, and the large glass window comes with plastic tearaways so the glass itself won't become etched and clouded.

Media blasting takes a lot of air, so if you can afford a 5 hp compressor that puts out air at 80 pounds of pressure at the rate of at least 7 cubic feet a minute, don't scrimp here. You can get by with a 2 hp compressor, but it will run constantly. Generally, the more air power you have, the better you will do the job. You will also need to hook up a shop vacuum to the back of your cabinet to keep the view clear and to help equalize the pressure inside. Otherwise, the pressure from blasting inside the cabinet will force air and particles past the seals on the doors.

You will want to add a water and oil trap in the air line to your blast cabinet because moisture and oil will cause the blast media to clump, clogging your cabinet's siphoning tube, too. If

Reach-around welding grips are great for holding sheet metal panels in alignment while pop riveting them together.

Steve puts the finishing touches on the cabinet.

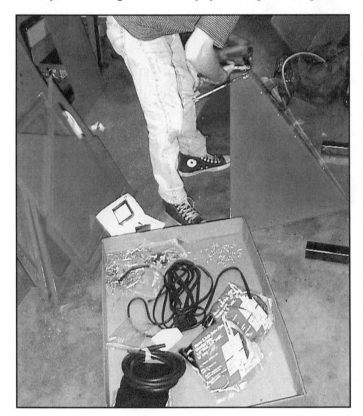

Blast cabinet kits can be purchased by mail order and sent UPS. They go together in a few hours.

Large side doors are attached and wire grid is dropped in before gloves are attached.

you live in a damp climate, you may even want to add two water traps, since compressing air causes the water to condense out of it.

Add a ground wire to your blast cabinet, too. All that abrasive media rushing through the tube generates static electricity that can give an operator quite a jolt. Just attach a wire to one of the frame bolts and run it to a water pipe or other metal ground.

TIPS AND TECHNIQUES

Media is a super way to get rid of rust, paint, and scale, but don't try to get dirt and grease off with it. Clean your parts with lacquer thinner or another solvent to make them free of grease and oil, and use a wire brush or putty knife to rid them of dirt and caked-on grunge.

You will also need to plug orifices and holes opening to the inside of mechanical parts, both to keep the

abrasive medium from damaging bearings, and to keep it from pitting polished surfaces. You can use masking or duct tape, or plastic plugs available from specialty houses.

Periodically you will want to sift your blast media to prevent clogs. Use a fine screen, and drain the medium from the bottom of the hopper into a fine-screen filter. You will also want to put your blaster in a dry place, not under a carport outside.

Finished cabinet ready for blasting. All you need is a shop vacuum and an air supply.

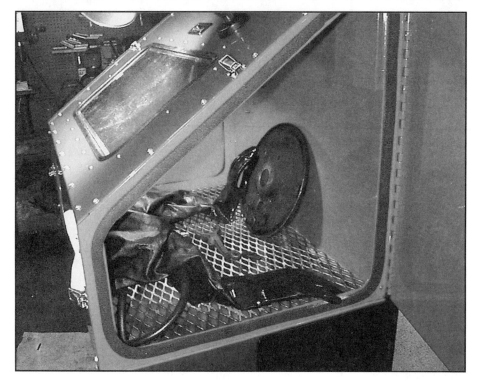

We loaded a few parts inside for the blast off.

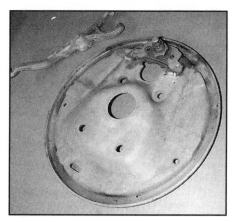

With a few minutes' work our parts came out clean as a whistle, ready for a metal etching wash and paint or powder coating.

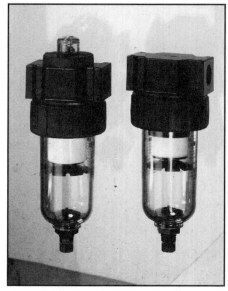

Moisture and oil separators. The closer you mount the moisture separator (pictured on the right) to the end of the line, the more effectively it will remove moisture.

These vinyl caps and plugs, from Eastwood, work great for keeping grit or paint out of critical tolerance areas, and they're reusable.

Which medium you use depends on what you want to do. Surprisingly, sand itself is not used in blast cabinets, or for much of anything other than removing graffiti anymore. It is very aggressive, but doesn't recycle well as it tends to fracture on impact, and the dust from it can cause silicosis. Here are the most popular media and their intended uses:

GLASS BEADS

This is the most common general purpose abrasive. It works well on all types of metals and plastics and is inexpensive. It is great for softer metals such as aluminum pistons, and engine blocks, and for light rust removal on harder metals. Not recommended for heavy rust removal.

Originally used on road signs, glass beads produce a satin sheen on aluminum and brass.

ALUMINUM OXIDE

This is the longest lasting rust removing medium. It's great for blasting rust from cast-iron manifolds, water pumps, and bell housings. You would not want to use it on plastics, however.

Aluminum oxide is the most popular rust remover. Be sure to wire brush any areas to be welded, brazed, or soldered to remove aluminum residue.

SILICONE CARBIDE

Silicone carbide has very sharp edges, making it ideal for blasting off heavy rust. It is also especially good for welding and brazing prep. It is about twice the cost of glass beads or aluminum oxide, though.

Silicon carbide is fast cutting but doesn't last as long as aluminum oxide.

WALNUT SHELLS

Walnut shell media was first used on military aircraft parts because it cleans well without damaging most surfaces, and the dust left over will break down rather than ruin bearings.

Walnut shells are ideal for removing internal engine carbon deposits during a rebuild.

POLY ABRASIVE

This will not harm fragile surfaces and produces little dust. It's great for stripping paint from sheet metal and fiberglass, though it is pretty expensive at around $100 for a 50-pound bag.

Poly abrasive is the most effective media for the removal of paint or powder coating.

Engine & Chassis DETAILING
Powder Coating

That's right. Now you can powder coat in your garage or home workshop. It's less trouble than painting, the coating is beautiful and nearly indestructible, and the equipment for the job isn't expensive. You can coat engine accessories, suspension and steering components, engine and transmission castings, and just about anything else made of metal that will fit in an oven.

The new powder-coating system uses lower voltage and is simpler and less expensive than professional systems. The rig retails for $149, and a can of powder in any of more than 40 colors, as well as a satin or a gloss clear, will set you back $9.99. That's not much more than the $135 it would cost to have a pro powder coat an intake manifold and a couple of valve covers for a small-block V-8. The quality and durability of the finish is just as good. The difference is, when you're finished, you own the equipment and can use it any time you choose.

When I found out about Eastwood's new system, I had them ship me one

by express delivery so I could finish my pickup chassis. This system is actually less messy and less toxic than painting. Powder coating produces nuisance gases during the curing process and puts a little particulate matter into the air during the coating process, but there is no overspray and no toxic vapor. Yet it produces a finish far superior to paint and you can dispose of the unused powder in the trash without violating environmental laws.

Powder coating was invented 40 years ago and became popular in Europe in the 1970s due to efforts to cut down on volatile organic compound (VOC) emissions. Here's how it works: The part to be coated is grounded, then the electrically charged plastic powder is shot onto it. The powder clings tightly to the part because of the charge. Then the item is baked in an oven at 400 F degrees for 15 to 30 minutes, depending on the size of the part.

When the component cools, it looks like it has a nice coat of enamel-but

it's much better because, unlike ordinary paint that can be scratched or damaged by solvents, this stuff is impervious. It's more durable that the best urethane products. If you ever need to remove it, apply copious amounts of heavy-duty paint stripper and leave it in a plastic bag overnight.

The tool used to shoot on the powder runs on ordinary 110-volt household current and puts out a charge of more than 9,000 DC volts. Though it could be unpleasant if you ran afoul of the tip, the shock won't harm you because it is like those you get from walking on cheap carpeting on a dry day. You might not want to zap yourself if you wear a heart pacemaker, but the gun itself is not dangerous. Treat it with respect as you would any electrical tool.

You also need a supply of compressed air that puts out a consistent 5 to 10 pounds of pressure. More than that will damage the coating equipment, so if you have a large compressor, use a regulator valve. Make sure you use the water trap provided, or a good set of professional water traps such as those used for paint spraying. You may want to order extra water traps. They need to be changed fairly frequently (every couple of weeks in regular use) to avoid pits in the coating.

For curing components, I purchased an old electric stove. Because my garage is wired for 220 volts, hooking it up wasn't a problem. I don't recommend curing parts in a gas oven because of the possible flammable nature of the powder, but I do intend to experiment with an electric heat gun in the near future. Your spouse won't want you curing components in the kitchen oven due to the gases and odors the process gives off. Also, your steaks may taste pretty bad!

CLEAN IT UP

To powder coat components, prepare them as if you were going to paint them. In the case of chassis parts, you can media blast them clean. For delicate sheet-metal parts, strip them using paint stripper or four cans of Drano crystal drain cleaner in 10 gallons of hot water, then degrease, derust, and etch them using a rust remover and cleaner like Oxysolv. If you are powder coating a thick, porous, new or used, cast-iron or aluminum casting you will need to do a preheat and extra cleaning to make sure no oil or grease is left in the pores.

Here's how it's done: First, strip the part using a media blaster. (I like to use glass beads because they are not as aggressive as sand, yet they do a good job of paint and rust removal. Use aluminum oxide for heavier rust, as the glass beads can peen clean metal over rusty pits.) When you have the part stripped to clean metal, place it in an oven preheated to 400 F degrees for five to 10 minutes (big parts, such as bell housings, take longer) to get the oil and grease in the pores of the metal to bubble to the surface. Then let the part cool a little and clean it with a good degreaser. Keep repeating this process until no more oil seeps out. (This would be the ideal way to clean a casting in preparation for painting, too!)

From here on, handle your parts using nitrile gloves to prevent skin oils

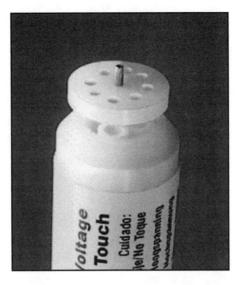
The High Performance Deflector (Part No. 10128) does a good job coating large areas with greatly improved transfer efficiencies.

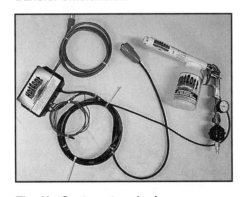
The HotCoat system looks more complex than it is. The powder gun is at right, the actuation switch is in the middle, the ground wire is at upper left, and the power supply is at lower left.

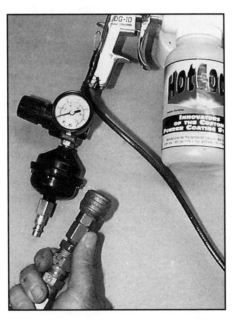
A regulator valve and water trap are musts, as is a modest compressed-air supply. Pressure needs to be 5-10 pounds; more could damage the gun.

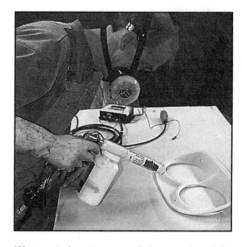

Parts need to be stripped of paint and rust, then treated with a good metal prep such as Oxysolv or PRE Painting Prep.

Powder is nontoxic and comes in more than 40 colors. You need at least an inch of it in the canister to powder coat. Fill the cup about one-third full for a typical job.

Wear at least a particle mask while shooting powder, and keep the gun moving about 3-4 inches from the part. Coat recessed areas with the Standard Deflector, letting the peripheral spray fall into recessed areas.

from contaminating them. Also, once you've cleaned the part completely, coat it as soon as possible to avoid flashover rust. Before shooting the coating, wrap bolt threads or areas you don't want coated, such as machined surfaces, with high-temperature tape. (You can also use ordinary masking tape, which will get a little crispy but won't burn, and aluminum foil works very well.) It's best to remove regular masking tape before curing to save cleaning up the adhesive residue. If you powder coat threads and machined surfaces, they will be thicker and won't go back together readily.

SHOOT THE POWDER

For this next step, wear a mask. If you have a mustache or a beard, as I do, smear a little Vaseline around the edge of the mask to help it seal. Shooting the powder requires a paper-particle mask, but the curing process will require a respirator. The resulting fumes are not nearly as toxic as two-stage Imrons, but you don't want to breathe them.

Also, before powdering your parts, make wire S-hooks from old, unpainted coat hanger wire, just as you would if you were going to hang a component for painting. Use these hooks to carry the parts without touching the powder and suspend it

from your oven racks. Arrange the oven racks so the part will be suspended without the powder touching anything, then preheat the oven to 400 F degrees. Use an oven thermometer to verify the temperature.

Finally, fill the powder cup in the gun about one-third full in the color of your choice. There are more than 40 colors and coatings to choose from, including two clear-coats and natural aluminum. Most of the colors echo the aerosol paints used in underhood restoration. By the way, some translucent colors are spectacular on polished-metal surfaces.

Now you're ready to start shooting. Clip the ground wire to the part, then depress the actuation switch

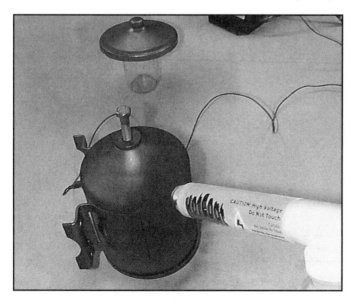

Powder clings to parts well, but it must not be touched until it is cured.

The powder cures in 15 minutes at 400 F degrees, but make sure you wait for the powder to "flow out" or gloss over before you start the timer. Allow parts to cool 15-30 minutes before installing.

and begin. First apply the powder into recessed or inside corners. Point the gun "across" the surface, not directly "at" the surface. Shoot quickly, because if you linger in one spot, a Faraday cage effect can develop in which the electrons will repel the powder, causing inconsistency.

Once you've coated the recessed areas, point the gun at the surface and coat the balance of the piece. Keep the nozzle about 3-4 inches from the part as you shoot. Getting too close will cause a spark to discharge. Inspect your work with a high-intensity lamp. When you have coated it to your satisfaction, undo the ground clip and touch up the little bare spot it leaves with a short burst of powder.

You may experience a situation where the powder tends to build up on raised surfaces, yet avoids recesses. If so, position the part with the crevice up so that gravity pulls the powder down into it. If you mess up the process, blow off the powder and start again. Gently pick up your part using needle-nose pliers to grip its S hooks, then hang it from a rack in your oven. The powder clings to the part, but it will come off if you touch it, sort of like the scales on a butterfly's wing. Close the oven door and "bake" the component for the full 15 minutes after the powder flows out (appears liquid).

When the time is up, let the part cool for 20 minutes with the oven off and the oven door partially open. Put on heavy gloves or use pot holders to lift your part out by the S-hooks. Your component will look great, stand up to road grime, flying stones, and solvents, and the finish will last for years. You can use this powder coating tool for engine accessories such as air cleaners, intake manifolds, valve covers, pulleys, master cylinders, battery boxes, bell housings, suspension parts, brake backing plates, even wheels. Your only limitation is the size of the oven.

TROUBLESHOOTING

CONTAMINATED POWDER:

Make sure gun is thoroughly cleaned before changing to another powder to avoid specks of the previous color in your new finish.

COATING POROUS MATERIALS:

Contaminants in porous materials will cause pits in the finish. If this happens, remove the powder coat with paint stripper or plastic media, rinse it with water, and spray with metal prep. Porous cast iron, cast aluminum, and magnesium parts can trap contaminants that will expel gas and cause pitting problems when the powder cures.

PREHEATING:

To prevent porosity problems, preheat the part. The time a parts needs to be preheated varies with its size. The oven needs to be between 200 and 400 F degrees. Use a painting prep to remove the bubbling contaminants. Wipe the part until no further dirt comes off on a clean white rag. Coat problem parts while they are hot. If pitting problems continue, remove the failed coating with stripper, then preheat the part to 250-300 F degrees again. Quickly remove the part from the oven and apply powder. After the part is coated, immediately put it back in the oven to cure normally at 400 F degrees.

ORANGE PEEL:

Some orange peel is unavoidable, especially with polyester-based powders. An orange-peel condition often can be leveled by sanding the part with No. 400 or finer grit sandpaper (wet or dry), then using a loose-section buffing wheel with white rouge compound to develop a high luster. Keep the part moving to avoid melting the coating.

EXCESS POWDER BUILDUP:

Another cause of rough finish is excess powder buildup. You will know if powder buildup occurs because the powder will start to stand on end like hair. If this happens, stop applying powder and blow off the excess. If powder does not apply evenly due to moisture buildup, replace the moisture trap on the gun and use fresh powder.

MOISTURE:

If the gun does not spray, the air pressure could be too low because moisture is clogging the disposable filter. The level of powder in the cup should be at least 1 inch in order to flow efficiently through the gun. Try gently shaking the gun as you apply the powder.

The coating can be removed using Aircraft and Automotive Paint Remover. Powder coatings are much more solvent-resistant than other coatings and require more time than paint to remove. To speed results, cover the part with a heavy coating of remover and place in a plastic bag to prevent evaporation. You can also used a heat gun and scraper to remove the coating, or Poly Abrasive. You may be able to remove residual powder coating left behind by strippers with conventional abrasives.

TIPS ON CARE OF POWDER-COATED SURFACES

- Powder-coated surfaces shed dirt easily. Wash with a mild detergent and water solution.

- Automotive paint polish may be used to remove water spotting and enhance the gloss.

Engine & Chassis DETAILING

Spraying Paint

Shooting paint, whether onto a chassis, an accessory, or on your car's body requires practice and good habits, but anyone with a little patience can do it. With the new High Volume, Low Pressure (HVLP) systems, it's not as messy as it used to be. But even with HVLP equipment, keep in mind that some types of paint are more toxic than others, The most toxic, such as Imron and the urethanes — even gloss-hardener additives in enamels — should only be sprayed in a professional booth wearing a fresh air pack.

More importantly, work in a well-ventilated place that has fans with special, flash-proof motors. The motors in ordinary fans give off sparks in operation, and because a spray gun works much like a carburetor in that it atomizes volatile fluids, the combination creates a potentially explosive situation.

You will also need adequate light, so install a few fluorescent fixtures (you can buy them at Home Depot for a nominal price) on the ceiling and the walls of the shop. These are especially critical — if you are working

indoors — for shooting the kinds of dark colors used on most chassis.

Make sure the work area is spotlessly clean of dust and contaminates. Vacuum out the whole work area. Wash or mop down the floor in your painting area making sure it is dry before using anything electric, because you could get shocked. Also, standing water on a floor can be blown into wet paint and cause fisheyes and corrosion.

Never work where there is a water heater or other device where a pilot light could set off fumes. And — this bears repeating — if you are an amateur, stay away from horribly toxic two-stage paints like Imron. (If you really want to shoot Imron, rent a spray booth, get a fresh air pack, and use the safety devices religiously. The stuff is deadly.)

EQUIPMENT

Until recently, the standard rig most pros used for spray painting was at least a two-horsepower compressor, a couple of water traps, 50 feet of hose,

and a couple of good spray guns. At today's prices, this equipment could set you back $800 to $1000. And yes, these items are still available and will do a marvelous job. The problem is, the old-style guns actually put less than 50 percent of the paint on the car. The rest winds up in the air and on you. Thankfully, now there is a better way.

A few years ago, manufacturers were looking for means to cut down on the toxic and dangerous pollutants pumped into the atmosphere by spray painting. What they came up with was the high-volume, low-pressure system. It consists of an electric, three-stage turbine that looks like a square, canister vacuum cleaner with a paper air filter on its side, 30 feet of clear 1-inch diameter hose, and an almost conventional looking spray gun. (Its spray orifices are a little bigger, and the gun is somewhat lighter than a conventional gun.)

There is no compressor involved, and there are no water traps. There is no need for either of them. I use a model called the AccuSpray that sells at this writing for $895. I like it because, once used to it, the rig does as good a job as old-style equipment. It also meets the newest federal Volatile Organic Compounds (VOC) regulations, which is important to me because in California, where I live, HVLP systems are the only legal systems. I also like the fact that an HVLP system takes one-third less of the $90-a-gallon paint to do a car.

Just because your painting rig meets VOC regulations does not mean it is legal to paint the chassis in your garage or driveway. Be sure to check with local authorities before setting up a home spray booth or shooting lots of paint outdoors. If you are not allowed to paint in your area, check with local junior colleges to see if you can use their auto shop spray booth. Better yet, enroll in a night class. Another possibility is to check with local body shops to see if you can rent their spray booth on weekends.

MIXING

Combine paint and reducer carefully to the exact measurements called for in the instructions. (To avoid liability problems, some manufacturers no longer put mixing instructions on paint cans. But they will send you a flyer that includes mixing directions if you call or write for one.) Stir the paint thoroughly, then strain it through a disposable paint strainer provided as a courtesy by most automotive paint stores.

The best way to learn how to spray paint is to practice. Nobody does it right the first time. Get some old tin cans, lawn furniture, bad body panels or discarded barbecue hoods and practice shooting various surfaces before shooting your classic's carefully prepared components. The spray gun should be held as close as 3-4 inches from your work. The nozzle should be perpendicular to the object you are painting. If you angle the gun toward the surface, more paint will build on the near side of the circle of spray than the far one, causing runs.

Set pressure and volume with the controls on the back of the spray-gun handle according to the instructions that come with the paint, or those that came with the equipment. Different

Many restorers have switched to HVLP spray equipment. This is the complete rig. There are no water traps or big compressors required. An HVLP system puts more of the paint on the car and less into the air than the old style equipment, too.

On the left is a high-quality Binks spray gun, the mainstay of every auto painter's spray equipment for 50 years. In the center is a new HVLP gun. Its head and orifices are bigger because of the lower pressure and the higher paint volume. On the right is an inexpensive foreign-made spray gun. In the past, many pros shot primer with one of these, then used the expensive Binks or De Vilbiss guns to shoot color coats.

If you choose to go with traditional equipment, you'll need at least a two-horsepower compressor. This one is mounted high so water condensed out of the compressed air can be drained off easily.

TIPS FOR PAINTING WITH AEROSOL SPRAY CANS

Items such as springs and axles can easily and conveniently be painted using aerosol paint cans. The results will hold up and look good if you follow these suggestions:

• Buy quality paint that is intended for the purpose (engine block, manifolds, etc.). Also, pick up a few extra spray tips while you are at the paint store.

• Always shake the can thoroughly before spraying. "Thoroughly" means two full minutes of shaking. That may sound excessive, but many paints have heavy pigments in them that settle to the bottom of the can in storage. If you don't shake the can well enough, the spray tip will clog in no time.

• Take the same safety precautions with aerosols as you do with a spray rig. Wear a charcoal mask, work in a ventilated area, and don't work near a potential source of combustion.

• Just as with a spray rig, if you are shooting enamel, shoot on a light, misty, tack coat and let it get sticky before shooting on a heavy coat.

• Don't let up on the nozzle between passes to prevent the tip from clogging and sputtering. Also, when a can is running out of paint, don't try to shoot every last drop. You'll get splatters and runs if you do.

• Before putting a half-empty spray can away for later use, turn it upside down and depress the nozzle until gas comes out clear. This will prevent the nozzle from clogging with dried paint.

Traditional systems also require water traps (two are preferable) in the air lines to your gun to avoid shooting water into your paint.

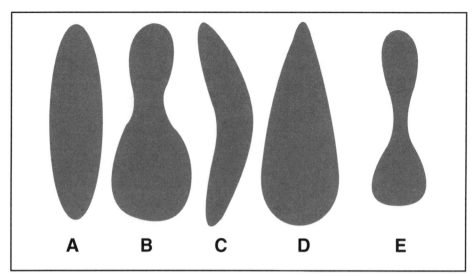

A B C D E

A is how your spray pattern should look. B indicates that atomizing pressure is too low. Increase pressure at gun, or with old-style systems, at the compressor. C is the result you get when the spray pattern is skewed to the right or left. Usually this is because a wing port on the air cap is clogged. Example D shows a pattern big at the bottom, but this can also occur with a big top. This is due to a partial clog in the spray nozzle. E shows a spray pattern that is squeezed in the middle which means the atomizing pressure is too high (a problem often experienced with old-style equipment).

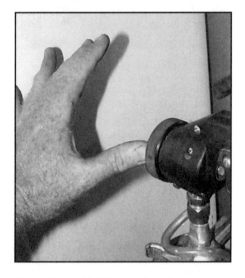

No matter which type of equipment you use, hold the spray gun 3-4 inches from your work while shooting.

types of paint require different pressure and volume settings. While painting, don't let up on the trigger between passes. Doing so increases the chance of a clogged gun. Overlap your passes by about one-third to insure even coverage.

Another little trick when shooting enamel is to first shoot on a fine mist, let it get tacky, then shoot on a nice, wet coat. That way you avoid sags or runs. The object-and the challenge-of spray painting is to shoot on as wet a coat of paint as possible without causing sags. However, if sags form, let

them alone until the paint dries, then sand them out. Trying to wipe them off with a rag will make a bigger mess.

When you finish shooting, take your gun apart and clean it thoroughly with lacquer thinner. Use lacquer-soaked pipe cleaners to get into the pickup tubing and use toothpicks to clean spray and vent orifices. Never use wire to clean nozzles or orifices because the surfaces are carefully machined and can be ruined with harsh treatment.

Cleanup is very important because most problems with sputtering spray

Disassemble your spray gun and clean all of its parts thoroughly in lacquer thinner after each use. Clean the spray nozzle with a toothpick soaked in lacquer thinner. Never use wires or pins for this job because they will ruin the carefully machined nozzle surfaces.

Use lacquer thinner-soaked pipe cleaners to scrub out the tubes in your spray gun before putting it away.

Lower adjustment is fluid-to-air mixture control.

Upper adjustment is air pressure. On an HVLP gun this usually is set at maximum, which is 5 to 7 pounds.

guns can be traced to sloppy maintenance. That includes leaving bits of dried paint in the wrong places. Finally, put a little Vaseline (do not use any lubricant containing silicon) on the volume-adjuster needle shaft where it enters the packing gland to help it seal before reassembly.

Above all, don't just shoot first and ask questions later. Patience is a virtue for a beginning painter. If you are unsure of anything, call the paint store where you purchased the materials, or call the manufacturer and clear up your confusion.

AEROSOL PAINTING PITFALLS

Whether you are using a professional-quality spray rig or an aerosol can, similar problems can occur. Here are eight common problems and what to do if you run into them, courtesy of the Eastwood Company:

DRY SPRAY

Problem: Dry paint dust settling over previously painted areas.
Causes: Paint drying too quickly; work piece too large to paint with an aerosol; application too slow; spray can is too far from surface.
Repair: Sand with fine-grit sandpaper followed by compounding and polishing or refinish as required.

BLISTERING

Problem: Bubbly, pitted, or swollen appearance.
Causes: Trapped solvents; painting over dirt or moisture; rust under surface.
Repair: Sand and refinish; if necessary, sand to bare metal. Ensure surface is completely clean before repainting. Allow sufficient "flash time" (the time between coats) to allow solvents to evaporate — usually 15 to 20 minutes.

RUNS OR SAGS

Problem: Coating doesn't adhere uniformly to the surface being painted.
Causes: Paint drying too slowly; sprayed over wax, oil, or grease; finishing coats too heavy; paint can or work surface too hot or too cold.
Repair: If wet, use a camel's-hair brush to brush out sag and recoat surface. If dry, sand with fine-grit paper, then compound and polish; or refinish.

ORANGE PEEL

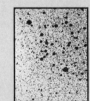

Problem: Surface looks like the skin of an orange.
Causes: Paint can held too far from surface; shop temperature too high (for best results, apply paints between 65 and 75F degrees.) Spray nozzle clogged.
Repair: Sand with fine-grit sandpaper (600 or finer) and use a fine compound to rub out orange peel. If this fails, remove paint and refinish.

SPITTING

Problem: Little or no paint coming from nozzle.
Causes: Nozzle obstructed or clogged; valve clogged.
Repair: Remove nozzle from can and put several drops of lacquer thinner in valve. Do not poke or pick at valve. Soak nozzle in lacquer thinner for a few seconds. Replace nozzle in can with slight twisting motion. Do not push nozzle straight down into can.

MOTTLED SURFACE

Problem: Uneven appearance (generally affects metallics).
Causes: Paint can not shaken enough; paint can held too close to surface; surface too hot or cold; can nearly empty.
Repair: Respray as required, using a swirling or rotating motion while spraying to deposit the metallic particles evenly on surface.

FISHEYES

Problem: Small, crater-like blemishes in the finish.
Causes: Paint can not shaken enough; improperly cleaned work piece.
Repair: If still wet, wash off paint. Thoroughly reclean and prep surface.

LIFTING OR WRINKLING

Problem: A swelling of wet film.
Causes: Improper drying of previous coat. Applying lacquer over enamel.
Repair: Material must be removed and the surface resprayed. Check content of top coat and substrate coatings before reapplying paint.

Engine & Chassis DETAILING
Welding Basics

I spent the first evening of an oxy-acetylene welding class I took many years ago burning holes in sheet-metal coupons that were a few inches square. We were learning to puddle the surface of these little steel plates without melting through them, and I wasn't too hot at it, no pun intended. In my first futile efforts I gained some perspective on why gas welding required a semester class at the local junior college. It wasn't easy to master and there was a lot you needed to know if you wanted to do it right.

Toward the end of the semester, one of my fellow students brought up the subject of MIG welding. "That's not real welding! Anyone could learn to do a passable job of MIG welding in a few hours," the instructor said with disdain. He obviously did not regard people who used MIG machines as welders at all. But whether he was right or not, nowadays there is a MIG welder in every auto repair shop from San Diego to Bangor because they are so easy to use.

The fact is, as he said, you can learn to MIG weld in a few hours. And if all you want to do is patch your car's unit body or chassis as needed, you won't need to know all that other stuff. A nice home-use rig like the Lincoln MIG-Pak 10 will set you back about $475 at this writing, and you can easily spend that much having your welding work done by a pro.

MIG, or Metal-Inert-Gas welding, is a form of electric arc welding. One version of the process is accomplished with the aid of a bottle of compressed, inert, shielding gas that surrounds the weld and prevents impurities from the atmosphere getting into it, while it also cools the surrounding metal. There is a similar technology that uses a special innershield wire that produces its own shielding gas. Lincoln wire-feed welders work with either system, though the setup with the separate gas bottle is the easier to master.

The wires used in wire-feed welders are called consumables because they are consumed when they are melted into the weld to fuse the two parts. (Welding can actually be accomplished simply by melting two pieces of similar metal together. This technique is called fusion weld-ing. It is not really useful to the home hobbiest, however.)

Consumables become part of the items to be welded together, so their composition must be tailored to the types of materials being welded. Mild steel, cast iron, aluminum, and stainless steel all require different types of welding wire. The thickness of the metal to be welded plays a part, too. Thicker metal requires thicker wire to achieve the penetration necessary to make a good weld.

Most of the welding you'll be doing during restoration will be on mild steel of various thicknesses. The type and size of wire you need will be specified in the instructions that come with your welder. In the case of the MIG Pak 10, there is a table inside the access flap covering the wire-feed spool that will tell you what to use for which applications and how to set the machine for best results.

GETTING STARTED

Welding isn't an exclusive pastime, but proper attire is required. You will want to wear cuffless

Lincoln's MIG Pak 10 from The Eastwood Company is versatile and one of the easiest welders to use.

trousers (blue jeans are good), because cuffs can trap red-hot sparks and embers and give you an unforgettable case of hot pants. A long-sleeved shirt is also a necessity to avoid being burned. And don't forget that welder's cap unless you fancy a red-hot shard embedded in your ear or scalp.

Also, never do any kind of arc welding without a full face-shield and proper protective lens. You can do permanent damage to your eyes in a hurry, and you'll get the worst sunburn you ever had if you neglect this item. Those fly-eye, wrap-around shades you picked up at the swap meet, perhaps for gas welding, won't protect your eyes at all, so don't use them no matter how cool you may look.

A dry, safe place is necessary. Never weld wet. That should be obvious. You and your clothes need to be dry, the floor needs to be dry, and the machine should never be used in wet conditions. Even with the household 115 volts that home welders use, a shock could kill you. Failing that, it can be damned unpleasant.

Your shop or work area should be well ventilated. Welding fumes are toxic, especially when welding galvanized surfaces. The area should be free of combustibles such as paint, solvent, or oil, and you should have a fire extinguisher close by. Never, never weld a

Inside a wire-feed welder is a roll of welding wire that is fed continuously as you weld. You adjust the rate to accommodate the gauge of the metal.

CHOOSING A WIRE-FEED SYSTEM

You should go with the MIG process if:

- Most of your welding is going to be done on 16-gauge or lighter metals.
- You can afford the extra expense and the lack of portability that a gas cylinder entails.
- You require clean, finished looking welds.

You should consider using the Innershield wire process if:

- You need simplicity and portability.
- You will be welding outdoors in windy conditions.
- You require good, all-position welding capability. (This could be important if you are going to be welding in floor patches on a unit-body car from underneath.)
- Most of your welding is going to be done on 16 gauge and heavier metals or on somewhat rusty or dirty metal.

THINGS YOU WILL NEED

A proper welding hood with the correct shielding lens. You'll need at least a No. 8 and preferably a No. 10 filter for MIG welding, and a No. 12 filter for Innershield, wire-feed welding. I use a Shade-master hood that you can see through easily, but automatically darkens when welding. These pro quality hoods are a bit pricey at around $165, though.

Heavy leather welder's gauntlet gloves. These should come well up your forearms and be thick enough to protect your skin from sparks and burns.

A welder's cap that comes down over your ears, with a flap for the back of your neck. They may look goofy, but such caps protect your pompadour from pyrotechnics.

Reach-around clamps. Ordinary Vice-grips will do in a pinch, but reach-around clamps make welding a lot easier. A set of clecos is also good for sheet metal.

Copper paddle for filling holes. It seems every old vehicle has holes in it somewhere that were used to mount long-gone accessories, or are there because of rust-out. A copper paddle is ideal for backing these holes and filling them in.

Gas bottle and gas. If you are going to be doing MIG welding, you will need to rent or buy a bottle of CO_2 or CO_2/argon shielding gas.

Welding cart. If you go for the MIG shielding gas, I'd recommend a cart for your equipment. It will make your rig a lot more portable and safer to use.

Wire cutters. These are needed to cut wire to length for the wire feed, or to cut sticks or electrodes to a usable size in some situations.

Welder's hammer. This is used for removing slag and cleaning up welds.

Scrap sheet metal on which to practice. An old fender or hood from an American car is good for this. Modern Japanese imports are made of thin, high-carbon steel, so their parts aren't suitable to practice on.

Practice welding on pieces of an old panel before you tackle your classic.

One setup is to use a bottle of inert gas such as an argon CO_2 blend to shield the weld and cool it. If you go this route, keep the bottle safely chained to a wall or your welding cart, and make sure to turn it off after each use. Leaking inert gas can displace the oxygen in a room, with dangerous results.

closed container! It will almost certainly explode.

A steel cookie tray with a 1/4-inch layer of sand is good to place under your work, or you can arrange several fire bricks on which to practice. Do not weld metal lying directly on a concrete floor, because rapid heat buildup can cause moisture in the concrete to explode violently! A steel work bench is nice, too, but not

required. Just remember, temperatures of 1200 to 1400 F degrees are required to melt steel, and that is more than enough to set most things alight, so be careful. Read and understand all of the manufacturer's manual before starting.

PRACTICE, PRACTICE, PRACTICE

Before you even think of attacking your resto project, you need to familiarize yourself with the technique. Just about anyone can learn to MIG weld with a few hours of playing around with the machine, but don't try to rush the process. A good weld must penetrate all the way through the pieces to be

joined. And a good weld also has a consistent look, sort of like a stack of dimes knocked on its side. It takes practice to be able to make these things happen, even with a MIG welder.

Get an old, crumpled hood or fender from the scrap heap at a body shop. Don't get a part from a modern Japanese import, though. Use a panel from an older American car instead, because the imports are often made of thin, high-carbon steel that is very hard to work with. Cut off some pieces about six inches square, and strip them of paint, rust, and grease. Welding should always be done on clean, healthy metal.

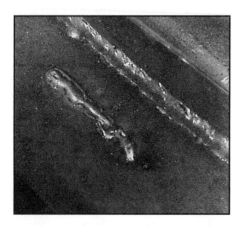

This is a beginner's weld. It is the result of moving too fast and is stringy and spotty, with little penetration. Above that is a good weld.

These two short welds are right. They are consistent, look like stacks of coins knocked on their sides, and penetrate all the way through the metal.

Butt welds should be done with the pieces to be joined about 1/32-in. apart to allow for heat expansion.

For your first attempts, just try to lay down a bead on the surface of the scrap metal. Adjust the wire feed and amperage according to the instructions that come with the welder. Lay your piece of scrap on the sand or fire bricks, then clamp on the ground lead. Extend the wire 3/8 to 1/2 in. If it sticks out too far, cut it to the correct length. Touch the wire to the work and squeeze the trigger. Hold the gun so the contact tip sticks out about 3/8-1/2 in. and draw it slowly away from the weld puddle at about a 45 degree angle.

If you are welding very thin sheet metal, you can go the opposite direction and push the nozzle away from the weld puddle at about the same angle, with the weld passing under your hand. This approach will help keep you from melting through.

The gap between the wire and the welding surface is important. The way you can tell if it is right is by listening to the sound of the welding. It should crackle, much like eggs frying. If your nozzle is too far away, you will hear a blowing or hissing sound. If you get too close, the wire may stick in your weld or in the nozzle.

Most beginning welders try to move too fast, creating a stringy, inconsistent bead with poor penetration. Let the metal puddle up as you go. I like to move the electrode in tiny circles as I work. This is not really necessary, but it helps me lay down a nice bead with thorough penetration. While welding, watch the puddle behind the arc, not the arc itself. It is the appearance of the puddle and the ridge where it solidifies that will tell you if your welding speed is correct. This ridge should be about 3/8-in. behind the electrode arc.

Make a few practice beads, then turn the scrap piece over and check the penetration. It should be a consistent line, with no gaps and no melt-through holes. Faulty welds can sometimes look great but be structurally unsound if they don't bond the two pieces completely together. Getting the penetration right is extremely important when working on a chassis or frame, because it can determine the future safety of your vehicle.

JOINED FOREVER

A good weld is actually stronger than the surrounding metal. A bad weld can be notoriously weak. Some types of welds are easier to do than others. Probably the easiest to do is a lap weld. A lap weld is when one piece overlaps another, and a bead is laid along one or both of the seams. Practice a few of these next.

When you have the lap weld down, try a few butt welds. A butt weld is when you weld two pieces of metal edge to edge. Leave about 1/32-in. gap between the two pieces to allow for expansion. Butt welds are the best approach to patching body sheet metal, because they leave no seams that can rust out from the inside, and because they can be ground flat.

Next you will want to do a few fillet welds. A fillet weld is used to join pieces of metal at right angles. Clamp the pieces in place, then lay a bead of weld along the seam, holding the welding tip at a 45 degree angle. Once again, good penetration is important. Welding that doesn't penetrate is called cold-casting and is quite weak.

When you have the fillet mastered, try a few edge welds with the metal back-to-back. These can be a bit of a challenge to do and still maintain a clean edge with no burning or melting. Finally, try doing corner welds. These are a very good way to join metal at right angles. Be sure the penetration is adequate and your welds are clean and consistent before going on.

If you are welding sheet metal panels, tack them together at both ends, then in the middle, then alternate welding back from each tack weld to avoid warps. The surest way to develop warps is to attempt

Joining two pieces at right angles with a fillet weld is done by holding the welder at a 45-degree angle to penetrate both surfaces equally.

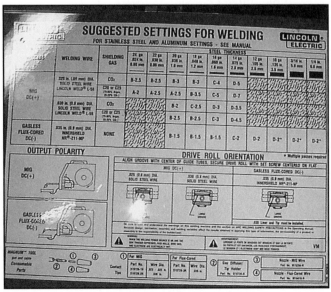

The Lincoln MIG welders have convenient instructions on the insides of their access panels to tell you which type and diameter wire to use with which kind of metal.

A less expensive alternative to the wire-feed welder is a stick welder such as this AC100 from The Eastwood Company. It can work even on sheet metal by coupling it with a stitch welder attachment. It takes a fair bit of practice to use one of these.

If you can't afford a MIG wire-feed welder, you can use the less expensive stick welders, such as the AC100 pictured nearby which uses welding sticks that look a lot like July 4 sparklers. They too produce their own shielding gas while welding. And with a stitch welding attachment, they let you weld even light sheet metal. They also work on household current, but they take a lot more practice to use. Without a stitch welder attachment, it would be impossible to weld thinner metal with a stick welder. The technique to weld with one of these is pretty similar to wire feed, except you need to get the hang of touching the electrode to the metal to make contact, then pulling it away from the work just far enough to develop an arc without the rod sticking to the base metal. Practice the scratch method and the touch method. Also, if you are welding light metal, push the electrode in front of you to prevent melt-through.

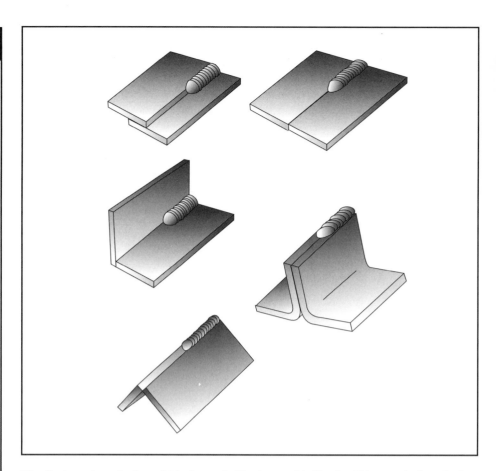

The first, and easiest, weld to learn is the lap weld. Master this one before trying the others. Next, practice the butt weld. It's the most useful for restoring body panels. Then try a fillet weld, an edge weld, and an angle weld. When you can do a clean job of these, with no melt-through and good penetration, you're ready to start on your chariot.

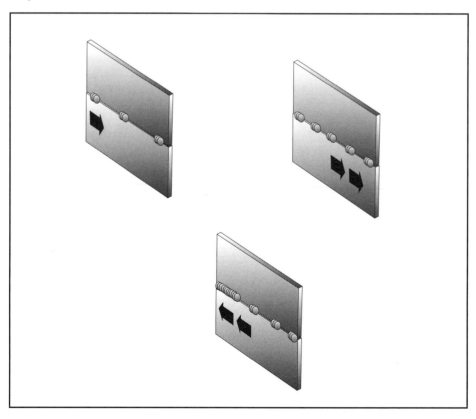

When welding thin sheet metal, tack it at each end first, then in the middle, and then at regular intervals. Work back from each tack weld to avoid heat distortion.

to just weld a straight line over a long span on light-gauge metal. Again, practice makes perfect.

My old instructor was right. Just because you can MIG-weld mild steel doesn't make you a welder. A welding certification takes a couple of years to obtain, and knowing how to do all the different types of welding on all the different types and thicknesses of metals takes a lot of time to master. But a MIG or stick outfit will solve most of your automotive welding problems. All it takes is practice, practice, practice.

Full face masks are a must for stick or MIG welding. The one on the left adjusts automatically to the amount of light and lets you see your work even when not welding.

Clecos are another convenient tool for holding pieces together and maintaining a consistent and correct gap between them.

TEN IMPORTANT SAFETY TIPS

1) In addition to eye and face protection, always wear protective leather gloves, a welder's hat, and a long-sleeved shirt. Don't wear pants with cuffs because sparks can shoot off of your work, lodge in your cuffs, and cause painful burns.

2) Never attach the ground clamp to, or try to weld on, a gas canister, a fuel tank (empty or not), or any pressurized container. Never attach the ground clamp to the bumper of your car, then weld in some other area. You can pit bearings and damage solid-state electronics if you do. Always place the ground clamp as close to where you intend to weld as possible.

3) Always weld in a dry area, in dry clothing, and make sure the leads from your welder are in good shape, with no breaks in the insulation. The voltage involved in arc welding is enough to injure or even kill. Never touch the live parts of your welder's electrode with bare skin or while wearing wet clothing.

4) Always turn off the CO2-argon gas bottle when you are finished welding. These gases, though inert, can displace the oxygen in a room with deadly consequences. They are odorless and have no taste, so you'd never know what hit you.

5) Keep your inert gas cylinder upright and chained in place so it cannot fall. If the valve is somehow knocked off, the bottle can take off like a rocket, with dangerous results. Never let the welder's electrode touch the gas cylinder, either.

6) Always weld in a well-ventilated place, using an exhaust fan if possible, and keep your face out of the fumes given off during the welding process.

7) Always make sure your welder is unplugged when changing polarity or changing wire rolls.

8) Always wear a proper face shield or welding hood equipped with a lens that provides sufficient protection for your eyes. You can do painful and permanent damage to your eyes if you don't. Sunglasses — no matter how dark — are useless as protection while welding.

9) Let parts cool before touching them with your bare hands. Welding temperatures can reach 1,200 to 1,400 F degrees, so parts can take longer than you think to cool down.

10) Always weld away from combustibles and keep an adequate fire extinguisher close at hand. Never weld in proximity with gas tanks, parts washers, paint cans, or oil and grease containers.

Busted Bolts

Busted bolts or stripped threads got you stumped? Neither situation is hopeless. Here's what to do. One of the most comforting sounds a mechanic can hear is the little squeak when a rusted, stuck bolt finally breaks loose. One of the nastiest is the awkward silence that occurs when the head of the bolt comes off, leaving a bright, shiny stub sticking out of your engine block or head.

What do you do next? Well . . . apart from throwing your hat on the floor, stomping around your shop, and uttering colorful language, there are a number of things you can try at home. Even if none of these strategies works, relax. There are guys who can get that bolt out for you. But more on that later.

UP-FRONT PREVENTION MEASURES

First of all, if you have a lot of rusted or stuck bolts to remove, shoot them liberally with penetrating oil and let it sink in for a day or so before you try to loosen them. Next, tap the bolt heads

with a ball-peen hammer. You don't have to hit them that hard, but you should set up a rapid tapping to break down the corrosion between the threads. Finally, if a bolt or two still won't turn, there is another good trick to try.

You can heat the bolt — but not the surrounding metal — using a propane or acetylene torch until it just starts to glow. You don't want to heat the surrounding metal because, if it is cast iron, the heat can make it brittle, causing it to crack. And with steel, you can change the molecular structure, causing it to become more prone to rust. Heating aluminum and brass will melt the metal if you aren't careful.

GETTING A GRIP ON IT

Okay, you've done all the above and you now have the head of one of those rusted bolts in your hand, its shaft still ensconced in the hole. If any kind of stub is sticking up, try turning it using Vise Grips and more penetrating oil. If the stud stays stuck, don't try to manhandle it — you'll break off what is left.

THE EASYOUT ROUTE

The next strategy is to drill a hole in the stub and tap in a bolt extractor. File the stub flat first, then use a prick-punch to make an indentation at the exact center of the bolt. Next, using a drill press if you have access to one, drill a hole in the exact center of the stub before installing the extractor. For best results, use one of Eastwood's left-hand drill bits, available in 1/8, 3/16, and 1/4-in. sizes. Often, the combination of heat generated and counterclockwise rotation is enough to back out the stud. You can try using a hand-held drill for this, but if you get the hole off-center or at an angle, you will probably break off the EasyOut when you try to turn it.

There are a couple of different types of bolt extractors, by the way. EasyOut is a brand name and is just one of the manufacturers of screw and bolt extractors. The first and most common type has a leftward spiral on it that you tighten into the hole made in the bolt to extract the stub. This style of extractor has the distinct disadvantage of compressing what's left of the bolt out against the threads of the hole, making the stub even harder to get out.

The other type of extractor has a square shank with a tapered blade that grips inside your drilled hole and helps you unscrew the bolt. This is the type pros use and the type I recommend. It compresses the bolt very little and does a better job than the spiral type. You also have a better chance of removing them if they snap. These professional-type extractors can be a little hard to find, but The Eastwood Company lists them in its catalog if you can't obtain them locally.

DESPERATE MEASURES

At this point you may be muttering, "It's too late, I already did that and broke off the extractor, too." Don't feel bad, I've done the same — more than once. When you break off the bolt extractor, your choices are limited, though the situation is not hopeless.

In the past I have attempted to drill the bolt and extractor out, and in doing so I damaged my drill bit on the hard extractor, ruining the threads of the hole. That's because bolt extractors are harder than drill bits and will destroy or deflect them, often causing damage to the casting in which the bolt is stuck.

There are two remaining approaches. You can try to find or make a very small hole saw out of hard steel tubing and then cut out the bolt from around the extractor using a drill press. Or you can locate a service similar to The Hole Shoppe in Signal Hill, California, which is owned by a fellow named Jim Thorpe.

Jim has been taking broken bolts out of holes for 25 years for oil drillers, machine shops, and aerospace companies and has dealt with every combination of iron, brass, aluminum, even plastic. He has a well-equipped shop that contains some state-of-the-art machinery for plying his rather specialized trade. One such machine looks like a giant drill press but is in fact nothing of the sort. It's actually a metal disintegrater.

In place of a drill bit it has an extremely high-voltage, low-amper-age electrode that is hollow and has water shooting down through it under pressure. The tip of the device dances up and down a few thousandths of an inch at a rapid rate and literally arcs, burns, and erodes the bolt away. It works much like a spark plug does over time. Ever notice how the electrodes on your plugs slowly burn away as a result of the high voltage current that flows across them?

This machine though, can burn a square, round, or even a hex-shaped hole in the bolt. Or it can erode the bolt away to virtually nothing. Best of all, its cooling blast of water prevents surrounding metal from heating up. So if you've got a tough one, The Hole Shoppe, and services like it in other parts of the country, can get it loose if you can't. If there is no service in your area, ship your part to Jim Thorpe's facility. He gets precious parts from all over the country, his fees are nominal, and he can do a quick turnaround if you need it. Call before sending anything. Contact:

The Hole Shoppe
J. D. Thorpe
3273 Grant St.
Signal Hill, CA 90604
Phone (562) 498-1446

FIXING DAMAGED THREADS

If you've messed up the threads in your part, all is still not lost. There are easy ways to remedy that situation, too. Here are a couple of good methods I picked up on a visit to Jim Thorpe's shop.

At the time, I was working on a '58 Chevy pickup and was close to setting the engine back in. In fact, it would have been in the truck but for a little problem. Screwed into the inside of the bell housing was a pivot ball for the clutch lever. When I took the throwout bearing arm assembly out to lubricate the mechanism, the ball fell out of its hole.

Thankfully there were still threads on the ball stud, and the ball did not look badly worn. But there were no threads in the bell housing for it to bite into. I couldn't figure it out. That's when I hastened to the Hole Shoppe. Jim Thorpe took one look at the situation and gave me the verdict.

Your first line of defense against busted bolts is penetrating oil. Squirt it on and let it soak in overnight.

Tap rapidly on stubborn bolts, preferably with a soft brass hammer so as not to damage the flats on the bolt head.

If penetrating oil and tapping on the head don't work, heat the bolt until red before wrenching. Be careful not to heat the surrounding metal.

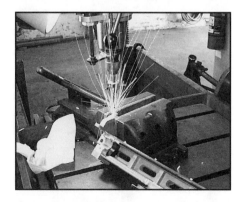

If all else fails, take your part to a shop with a metal disintegrater and have the stub eroded away.

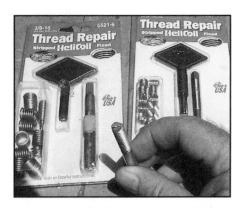

Some inexpensive thread-repair kits use a cheap plastic tool to install them. You can make a better tool out of a bolt by filing a notch into it.

This is a professional-quality tool for installing a HeliCoil. It holds the tang of the coil so you can twist the coil into the hole.

The first step to repairing damaged threads is to drill the hole out over-sized, preferably using a drill press.

Twist the coil in carefully until the tool bottoms out against the part.

A HeliCoil is in reality a diamond-shaped spring designed to compensate for the threads in the hole and the threads on the bolt that are to go into it. It is not a true thread, so you can't use an ordinary tap to put threads in the oversized hole. Nor can you use an ordinary tap to dress the threads inside a HeliCoil.

Next, using the tap that comes with the repair kit, make a set of threads for the coil to screw into. Clean the new threads, then cut the coil to the correct length by first counting the threads in the hole. Cut the coil to length using wire cutters.

Use the special tool supplied with the kit to screw the coil into place. Some kits come with only a plastic tool that can break when you try to use it. If you run into this problem, file a notch into a bolt with the correct threads for the inside of your coil and use it to install your insert instead.

Finally, use a punch to snap off the tang on the coil at the bottom of the hole used to tighten the coil into place. You now have a threaded hole in the correct, original size that will actually grip better than the original hole and bolt. If you are worried about the coil coming out, smear a little Loctite on it before installing it.

Another, similar system actually uses a threaded, solid insert. Once again, drill the hole out to the correct oversize, then twist a nut, followed by the insert, onto the correct-size original bolt. Tighten the nut against the insert, leaving a little of the bolt sticking out. After that, merely make sure the bolt is straight, then tighten the nut into the hole using an open-end wrench until the nut bottoms out. Break the nut loose while holding the bolt still. Finally, remove the nut and bolt from the new threads. The repair is complete. (Eastwood also carries a thread insert that works in a fashion similar to a HeliCoil. It is available in metric or standard sizes. And there are diagrams in the Eastwood catalog on how to install this item.)

Remember, anything can be fixed with the right tools and a little patience. By now you should have a couple of more devices in your mental tool box that will help you through the tough breaks every car buff faces.

After using the special tap needed to make new threads for your coil, count the threads in the hole so you can cut the coil from the top to fit the hole.

With the coil in place, you can now break off the tang using a punch.

A previous owner had heated the bell housing with a torch to extricate a worn pivot ball. In doing so, he had heat-treated the surrounding iron, making it brittle. (Cast iron is easily damaged by heat.) Later, continuous use caused the bell-housing threads to disintegrate. The only solution was to drill out the hole, make new threads, and install a thread repair insert. Here's how to do it:

HeliCoil is a popular brand of thread-repair system that uses a stainless steel spring. The spring can be screwed into an oversized hole to return it to its original size, creating a new set of threads in doing so. To install a HeliCoil, drill the damaged hole out to the correct oversize to accommodate the springlike coil. The company supplying the thread-repair system will tell you which size hole to drill.

Cut the coil to length using wire cutters.

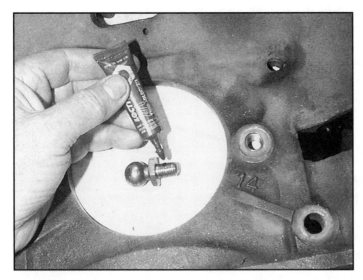

A HeliCoil grips better than the original threads, but if you don't trust it, use a little Loctite to make the assembly permanent.

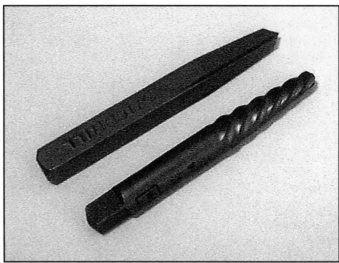

The spiral bolt extractor on the bottom is not as effective as the grooved one at top because it forces the broken bolt against the hole in which it is lodged.

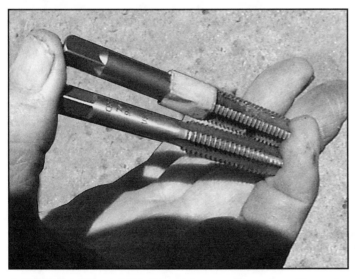

A HeliCoil tap is not the same as an ordinary tap. Use only the one that comes with the kit to tap a hole for your coil.

HeliCoils (left) are stainless-steel springs and don't have true threads, but there is another system that uses a threaded insert instead of a spring.

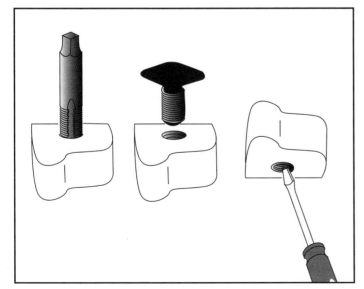

The usual coil thread repair involves drilling an oversized hole, tapping it with a special tap, then screwing in the springlike coil and breaking off the tang.

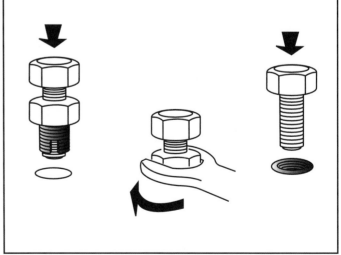

The insert type of thread repair also requires drilling out the hole, but no tap is needed since the insert is self tapping. An original-sized bolt and nut are used to install the insert. The nut is tightened until it bottoms against the surface of the hole. The bolt and nut are then unscrewed.

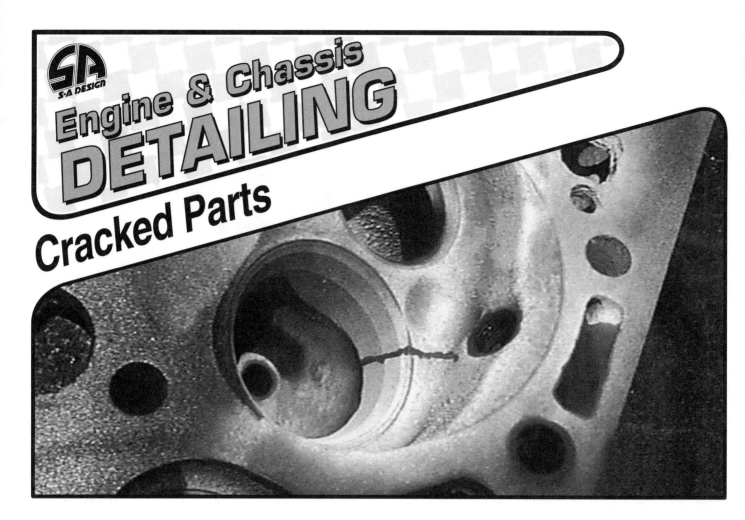

Engine & Chassis DETAILING
Cracked Parts

Engines, suspension components, axles, even frames, can crack under the stress of normal operation. Whenever you buy used replacements for such components, check them for cracks, preferably before handing over your money but certainly before installing them on your restoration project.

Until recently, that was easier said than done. Now there is a kit made by Magnaflux called the Spotcheck Jr. that makes the job easy. Magnaflux also came up with the original electromagnetic system that has been the standard and most thorough means of detecting cracks for many years. There are a couple of disadvantages to the old system, though.

For one thing, if you want to have parts Magnafluxed (the brand name has become the term for the process), you must take them to a machine shop since the equipment is not portable. The other limitation of the old method is that it only works on ferrous metals.

You can't use it to find cracks in aluminum or brass.

In contrast, the Spotcheck Jr. kit uses a dye and developer in aerosol vials instead of magnetic flux to find cracks, so it can detect them even in plastic. The whole kit, including a couple of containers of cleaner, is about the size of a cell phone. Take it with you to swap meets and salvage yards so as to check for problems before you lay down cash.

Here's how it's done. Shoot on the cleaner and wipe down the part with a rag to rid it of dirt, oil, and grease. The surface to be tested needs to be clean for the process to work. Shoot on a little of the red dye. (The aerosol canisters are color coded so you can't get confused.) Let the dye soak in for a couple of minutes.

Next, shoot a little of the cleaner onto your rag — not onto the part — and wipe off the dye. The reason you don't want to shoot the cleaner onto the part at this point is because it would cause the red

penetrant to diffuse, running further into small cracks. Now shoot on the white powder developer.

Even tiny, hairline cracks will become evident almost immediately as bright-red lines. Use a kit like the Spotcheck Jr. to check engine blocks, heads, rods, axles, gears, and frame joints, especially if there has been a collision or if the car has a lot of miles on it. If you are overhauling your classic's engine, it would be a good idea to have it checked the old-fashioned way, as well.

Cracks in cast iron or aluminum parts such as blocks, heads, and manifolds can sometimes be welded by professionals. But if replacements are available, they would be a better bet because of the damage heat can do to these metals. Cracks in connecting rods and axles should not be repaired. Replacements are the only safe alternative. Frame cracks can usually be welded safely.

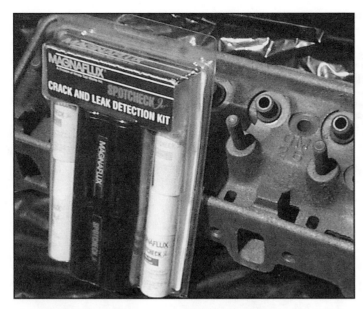

The Spotcheck Jr. kit from Magnaflux comes with a couple of containers of the cleaner plus one of the penetrant dye and one of the developer. The tips of the vials are color-coded for ease of use. A plastic holder and covers are included and make it convenient to take the kit to a swap meet.

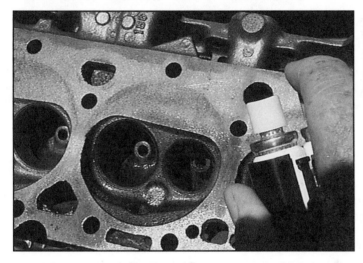

The part to be checked needs to be clean of oil, dirt, and scale. Just shoot on cleaner and wipe it off with a clean rag.

Next, shoot on the red penetrating dye and give it a couple of minutes to soak in.

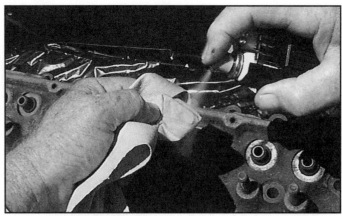

Wipe excess dye away by spraying the cleaner onto your cloth, then wiping off the penetrant. Don't shoot the cleaner directly onto the part.

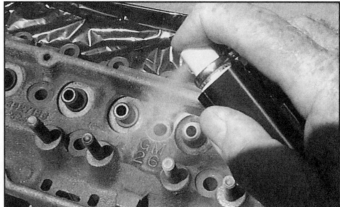

Finally, shoot on the white developer. Any cracks will show up almost immediately.

We found a sizable crack in the valve pocket of our Chev small-block, high-compression head. Repairs are possible, but a better bet would be to find another head.

We also found a hairline crack around this bolt hole in the top of the head.

Engine & Chassis DETAILING

Cleaning the Frame

This chapter assumes your car has a separate frame. Many more modern cars do not. If your car has a unit body, there are still some good tips in this section to help you toward that show winner. But the chapter on unit-body construction contains more details.

Yes it's a dirty job, but someone's got to do it. And unless you are Mr. or Ms. Megabucks, that someone probably has to be you. There is just no easy, clean way to do it. You can completely disassemble your car to its bare frame, then sandblast it clean, but this approach has its perils. For one thing, getting a body off a car, then back on without damaging or misaligning it is not easy.

Granted, a body off restoration is the only way to get at everything. But you can get at nearly everything without removing the body. When you finish your restoration, the doors will still hang right and the body will sit squarely on its chassis. It all depends on your skill level, and how ambitious you are.

Even if you don't want to take your car's body off its frame, you can still do a restoration capable of taking home the gold. However, you will need to do a lot of cleaning in hard-to-reach places. The only areas you won't be able to clean and paint will be the tops of the frame rails and the undersides of the body where it meets the frame rails.

I know these things from experience because the other day I had to really get down and dirty. Filthy, in fact, but I couldn't help it. You see, the only way to get a chassis clean is to get under and around it and start scraping and grinding. Even sandblasting, though great on rust, won't remove caked-on filth.

It's also true that items such as springs and suspension systems that are in good condition are often best left assembled, which makes cleaning them a real job. Perhaps, like me, you only want to clean your chassis and apply a show-quality finish without removing

every component. If so, you may want to try my time-tested recipe for transferring years of road grime from your restoration project onto your clothes and shop floor. First, assemble the following tools:

- **Putty knives**
- **Small squirt can**
- **Lacquer thinner**
- **Electric drill**
- **Assortment of wire wheels**
- **Sanding disk and sandpaper**
- **Strong twine**
- **Trisodium Phosphate (TSP)**
- **Scrub brushes**
- **Neoprene gloves**
- **Corroless Rusty Metal Primer**
- **Satin-finish black Corroless or Eastwood's Chassis Black**
- **Mechanic's creeper**
- **Jack stands**
- **Safety glasses and paper-particle masks**

Take your car to a car wash that has a pressure sprayer, lie down alongside it, and blast as much of the filth off of the chassis as you can. Alternatively, have your chassis steam-cleaned by services that specialize in that sort of thing or purchase a Grime Blaster that hooks to your compressor and a garden hose to do the job at home.

Don't blast the engine room. Lots of people do, but I don't like to use pressure guns or steam cleaners in engine compartments because of what they can do to hard-to-find distributors, generators, voltage regulators, and other electronics. These items can be damaged even when covered with plastic to keep moisture out. Also, I don't relish blowing dirty water into the engine's induction system.

Once you get all the loose stuff off with the blaster it's time to get serious by getting under. Before you begin, spread a heavy tarp on your driveway to catch the dirt, then drive or push the car onto the tarp. Put the vehicle up on jack stands so you can get beneath it easily, and remove the wheels so you can get to the brake backing plates. It's usually pretty dark under a car unless you have taken the body off, so it might be a good idea to put a brighter bulb in your trouble light to help you to see. Now put on some long-sleeved coveralls, a hat, and safety glasses, and roll underneath.

The worst stuff you'll have to deal with is the dirt-and-oil combination that forms a kind of

Here are tools of the trade. They're simple but the job is a dirty one.

tough, asphalt coating (often referred to in restoration circles by its technical name — gunk) wherever it sticks. Trying to dissolve it all with solvent is really messy, and steam cleaning and sandblasting doesn't seem to affect it appreciably. In fact, scraping it off with a sharp, stiff, putty knife is about the most effective approach. Scraping will remove most of it, and you can use sturdy twine to saw dirt from around bolts and other protrusions. Wire brushes help, as well.

Put a little lacquer thinner in your squirt can and use it on stubborn or hard-to-reach places to dissolve grease. Work outdoors or in a ventilated area and have a fire extinguisher handy. Lacquer thinner is volatile. Use old, absorbent rags to clean up your mess, and dispose of them properly so as not to risk a fire or pollute the environment.

When you get as much gunk off as possible, sweep it up so you won't track it everywhere. (This was my wife's idea.) Now put a stiff wire wheel in your electric drill and clean off as much of the rest of

Scraping off 40 years of filth is time-consuming but it IS necessary.

A wire wheel is great for getting rid of rust because it digs into pits.

The restorer didn't want to pull the body off the frame of this '39 Chev panel wagon. Doing so could easily tweak and deform the body. Pulling the front clip was easy enough and it allowed access to the dirtiest area of the chassis.

the dirt and rust as you can. There are several different shapes of wire wheels ranging from the fine, brass types to heavy-duty, twisted-steel brushes. You'll want an assortment of wheels for chassis cleaning because each has its own virtues.

When the wire brushes have done all they can do, install a sanding disk with No. 80 grit open-coat sandpaper in your drill and sand as much stubborn rust and discoloration off as you can. Areas that cannot be reached with your sanding disk will have to be done

by hand. This is a lot of work, but the cleaner the metal on your classic's chassis, the longer its new paint will last.

If your car's frame is boxed, it can be difficult to remove rust from the insides of the rails. Here is what I recommend: Rust converters usually require some degree of prep, and it's these areas that are typically impossible to prep effectively. I blow out loose dirt and debris, then gently heat the area to eliminate moisture. Using Eastwood's undercoating system with extension wands, I apply Heavy Duty Antirust. This waxy coating is not for areas that show because it is impossible to paint. But it cures very slowly, penetrating rust and into welds to effectively seal out moisture and air.

When you have everything as clean and bright as you can make it without becoming obsessive, you're ready to wash the chassis down. Pull the car off the tarp. Mix a strong solution of trisodium phosphate (TSP) and hot water, then put on neoprene gloves and goggles. Wash everything underneath, using scrub brushes from front to back to remove any remaining grease or oil. Rinse your work thoroughly with a garden hose.

When the chassis has dried, jack it up again and put it on jack stands. Remove the wheels. If you have a compressor and spray gun, mix up a pot of Eastwood's Corroless and shoot it on. Use big pieces of corrugated cardboard to shield fenders and running gear from overspray. Give the primer about 45 minutes to dry, then mix some of Eastwood's Chassis Black if you used Corroless primer. Use a touchup gun or an aerosol spray can of the same paint to get into tight places.

Let the frame dry at least 24 hours before resuming work. Corroless takes a while to dry, but when it finally does it is very tough and will last for years. The finish black is correct for most production cars and the results will surprise you.

The author's old hauler has a detailed chassis and engine at last. Now for paint and cosmetics.

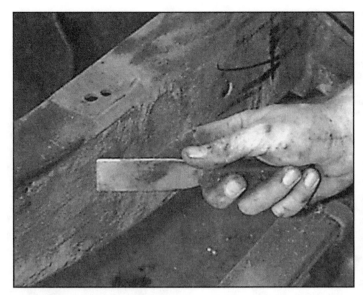

A sharp putty knife works well on heavy gunk.

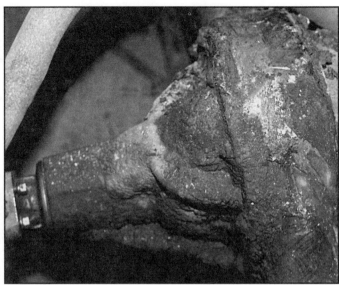

Not even sandblasting will remove built-up gunk like this. Scraping is the only answer.

Once the chassis is thoroughly cleaned, it's time for a coat of Eastwood's Corroless, followed by Chassis Black.

A well-detailed chassis includes cadmium-plated fasteners and cast-metal parts painted accordingly.

Painting your engine and frame to match the car can tie things all together very nicely.

This chassis is detailed, restored and clean enough to eat your lunch off.

Engine & Chassis DETAILING

S·A DESIGN

Rust Repair

Rust. The word sends a chill down every old car lover's spine. It can cost thousands to fix and can render an otherwise mechanically sound car unrepairable, unrestorable, and even undriveable. The best way to avoid having to deal with rust is not to buy a rusty car in the first place. But if you like old cars, chances are you'll end up paying for rust one way or the other, in any car you buy that is more than 20 years old.

I learned this all over again when I bought a little '67 Morris Minor a while back. Being from Southern California, I never thought much about rust unless it was obvious. This little Morrie looked good until we started stripping it for restoration. That's when I found out the thing was a tragedy waiting to happen.

That's because rust is most insidious in unit-bodied cars in which critical structural members can be compromised to the point where the vehicle is unsafe. Unit-bodied cars that look healthy and well maintained can actually be death traps

because of extensive rust. Before you buy any unit-bodied restoration candidate, you'll want to check its underside carefully for rot, rust, and poorly done repairs. Cheap, quick fixes with Bondo have no structural integrity at all and will actually attract moisture. Clumsily lap-welded repairs that aren't protected properly will just rust away that much faster, too.

Get under any prospective project car and poke around with a screwdriver or key. If the owner won't agree to this, let him keep his car. Take along a household refrigerator magnet and see if it sticks to sills, kick panels, the rear skirt under the trunk lid, and the floor pans. Don't use a powerful magnet for this, because it could actually stick to the car through 1/4-in. of plastic rebuild.

As we said, unless you can afford a freshly restored car or a pristine original, you will most likely have to deal with some rust on any old car. Luckily, there are several good strategies for ridding your car of it,

converting it, or at least arresting its progress.

Obviously, the best thing to do is to sand it off or cut it out and replace it with healthy metal. And if you are doing a frame-off restoration on a full-framed car, that won't be too big a problem. But if — like most of us — you don't want to go to that much trouble, or you can't afford to, or you're doing a unit-bodied car, there are some good techniques that will help stop the progress of corrosion and make your vehicle last for years.

CLEAN AND HEALTHY

The first line of defense against rust is to rid the underside of your car and your fender wells of dirt. Dirt soaks up moisture and salt and holds them against you car's precious tin where it will wreak havoc. A pressure cleaner or steam cleaner can be used to get it off, but don't shoot water inside the engine room. You could damage irreplaceable electrical components. Also,

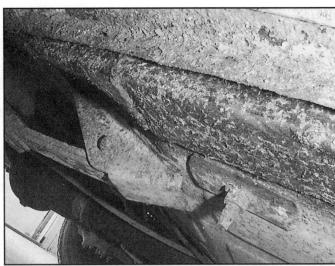

Unit-bodied cars depend on the integrity of their sheet metal for strength. Repairs with plastic filler like this may hide the problem, but they contribute nothing to structural integrity.

Spring hangers on unit-bodied cars are especially prone to stress. Rust gets a foothold in the cracks and a dangerous situation is the result.

once you do get your car restored, it is a good idea to wash the underside periodically to prevent problems, especially in wet climates and places where salt is used to thaw roads.

PATCHING PANELS AND CHANNELS

The bottom-line best way to eliminate rust from your classic is to cut it out and replace it. If your car is unit-bodied, it may be the only way to solve a significant rust problem. Each sheet metal panel of the structure of such a car helps support the others, so if any of them are unhealthy, the whole car can become unsafe. If floor pans and braces are rusted out, they will allow the car to twist and flex, causing metal fatigue and further problems. And a collision from the side in such a car could be deadly.

Replacing rusted sheet metal is not as difficult as it might seem, but read the welding chapter and practice a little if you are a novice at the art. Panels must be formed out of metal that is the same gauge (thickness) as the metal they replace, and they must be made of steel with the same carbon content as what they replace. (In the case of structural members, you may want to go to slightly thicker metal.) You can buy new metal or get healthy tin from a donor car. Usually, if you hit the metal with a pass from a surface grinder and it gives off sparks of the same color as the old metal, the carbon content will be right.

Make patterns from stiff card stock, and make sure they will fit before cutting up sheet metal. Patch panels can be formed using various tools — available from the Eastwood Company that fit in a vise and allow different types of bends. You can also use body hammers and a shot bag to shape compound curves. Butt welds are best for thin metal floor pans because lap welds — the alternative — create traps for moisture. Of course, some of the heavy

This rotted structural brace will have to be cut out and clean, new metal welded in. A job like this can be expensive if you have to pay to get it done.

Holes and old, poorly done patches mean plenty of work ahead for a restorer. Always test the underside of any restoration candidate by probing with a key or screwdriver to check for rust.

A whole new door pillar and much of the kick panel had to be welded in on this '67 Morris Minor convertible.

New structural braces were welded in to replace dangerously rotted ones. We used a heavier gauge metal for these, to give the little convertible extra rigidity.

structural pieces under a unit-bodied car are lap welded for extra strength. In that case, coat the inside of the new metal with Eastwood's cold galvanizing compound before welding it in. Cold galvanizing compound will not affect the weld and will protect the metal.

CONVERTING RUST TO CRUST

Nothing will make rust into healthy metal again. But you can convert the stuff to a benign substance called magnetite that does not rust. I like Eastwood's Corroless for this. It is especially good for hard-to-get-at places such as inside rear quarter panels and reinforcing structures. You only need to wire-brush the loose stuff off, then make sure the panel is free of grease and oil before applying it. You can brush it on in areas that won't show, or spray it in areas that will. Corroless also contains glass particles that interleaf during the curing process to help keep out moisture.

STOPPING RUST IN ITS TRACKS

There are places where the above solutions prove impossible or impractical, such as the insides of frame rails, and other areas that you cannot reach, between the frame and the body of a car, inside doors or rocker panels or other closed box sections. In those cases, a compound such as Eastwood's Heavy-Duty Anti-Rust is the answer. It forms a film over the rust that keeps moisture out and retards further corrosion. It is

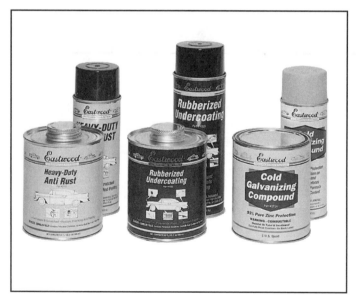

Eastwood makes a complete range of rust-fighting products that can make your car last years longer.

Eastwood's rust stabilizer is available in convenient aerosol cans for small jobs, or in larger containers for bigger tasks.

also self healing if it is nicked or scratched. It isn't suitable for areas that are directly exposed to the weather, but it is great for those difficult, sheltered places. There is even a special, long wand kit available for shooting this stuff in just such spots.

SEALING AND UNDERCOATING

Strip out and recaulk all seams on your car's structural metal. Caulk gets old, brittle and stiff from environmental contaminants and won't do its job. Also, unless you are going for a factory-fresh appearance on a car that you will be showing and driving only in fair weather, you might consider undercoating the chassis. Don't do the engine, transmission, driveshaft, or any of the steering components or grease fittings, but be sure to cover the sheet metal, especially in the wheel-well area.

These strategies, plus proper storage and maintenance will keep your car in pristine condition for years to come. Hose off the underside of your classic periodically to remove dirt and salt, and be sure to store your car indoors on a concrete or wooden floor, not earth as in a barn, because dirt attracts moisture that can condense on your car's underside and rot it.

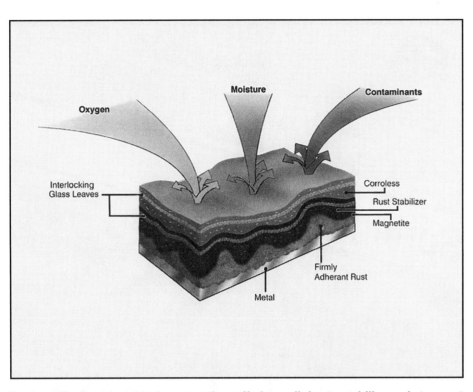

Eastwood's Corroless has been used on off-shore oil rigs to stabilize and stop rust in its tracks. It contains glass leaves that interlock and create an impermeable barrier against moisture

New sills and new kick panel mean doors will now hang correctly.

The author's little Morris Minor convertible looked pretty good at first glance, but there was a good reason why it was for sale for only $1,000.

Many of us, in our youths, were fond of abusing huge-engined American muscle cars for the glory we believed it brought us. Therefore, we know about spring failure. Most of the V-8s of the late '50s, '60s, and early '70s had more than enough torque to wrap up and snap their rear springs after a while. Those large-displacement V-8s were heavy because they were made of cast iron, so they eventually crushed the life out of the car's front springs, especially after repeated panic stops. If all that weren't enough, some of us did silly things to car springs.

We heated them and we sometimes cut them to lower our cars because we mistakenly believed that doing so would make our vehicles handle and look better. I was one of the worst offenders. Not only did I lower my own car but, at the age of 17, I kept myself in illicit beer and second-hand transmissions for an entire summer by lowering other people's cars. My constant companion was an acetylene torch. Typically, the deed was done by heating each

spring (leaf or coil) in one spot until it became bright red, then jumping on the car's bumper until the spring collapsed. This did terrible things to handling, ride, and steering geometry, but my customers rarely complained. We were all ignorant.

I'll admit it — I am a recovering spring abuser. But on my behalf I have spent the last 20 years trying to put as many old, battered derelicts back the way they were in an effort to pay for my misspent youth. It hasn't been easy. I am still occasionally tempted to do things I shouldn't, like pumping a little more power out of an old car's engine, or "improving" a car's appearance in ways that never occurred to the manufacturer's styling department. At this point I'm proud to say I have probably replaced or rebuilt nearly as many old car springs as I have destroyed. The task isn't too onerous.

Automotive springs are generally easy to remove and rebuild or replace. You can do the job with hand tools. If you are restoring a chassis, doing the springs can be worth the

trouble. New springs can make a big difference in the way your car rides. If you are an amateur restorer working at home, plan on a weekend for the front springs and another for the rears. What you need to do depends on how your car is configured; how it is configured depends on the era in which it was manufactured.

A LITTLE HISTORY

Cars until well into the 1930s and trucks into the 1950s generally followed buggy practice. They used leaf springs front and rear. Also, as often as not on antiques, there was only one spring in front and it was mounted transversely (across the car's frame). In fact, early Fords used transverse leaf springs front and rear that were semi-elliptic in shape. (They looked like the top half of an ellipse.) Ford continued this practice until 1948, even though other manufacturers had long since gone to more sophisticated approaches.

Surprisingly, early Ford suspensions worked pretty well, even though they were archaic by the 1940s. I had the opportunity to drive a '41 Ford recently and was surprised at how well it rode and cornered. It was certainly no worse than other cars of its era. Surprisingly, the Ford-type transverse leaf spring didn't entirely die in '48. Corvettes used them from 1964 until 1982 in their independent rear suspensions. But Corvettes are exceptions. Most cars made from the '40s until recently either used conventional coil springs in front and leaf springs in the rear or coils at all four corners.

FRONT COIL SPRINGS

Independent front suspension, with coil springs mounted in unequal A-shaped support (control) arms, has been the standard on American cars since the mid 1930s. This arrangement provides a better ride and better control than longitudinally mounted semi-elliptical leaf springs and solid axles.

Although the independent front suspension systems on most cars look complicated, they are simple to work on. Before removing the old springs from the chassis, make sure new ones are available. It is also crucial that you take the time to get the correct springs.

Most shop manuals list springs for the various models produced by the manufacturer for that year. There are a number of factors involved in determining which are the proper springs

THINGS YOU WILL NEED

- Wrenches, channel locks
- Jack stands (4)
- Spring compressor clamps
- Strong chain (4 feet)
- Leaf spring spreader (can be rented or made at home)
- Flat chisel and ball peen hammer
- Hydraulic floor jack
- Penetrating oil
- New springs (if required)
- Rubber spring pads (coil springs)
- Pin and rubber bushing set (leaf springs)

This front suspension is the earlier, kingpin-and-bushing type. Remove the pin at the top or bottom of the steering knuckle to remove the spring, though on some cars you need to drop the center of the A arm to get it out.

If you do nothing else on your chassis, make sure the rear axle is properly aligned and that the u-bolts are tight. Note the wrapped springs.

This hot rod chassis appears very simple, but looks are deceiving. Springs and shocks must be adequate for the weight of the engine and everything must be precisely aligned for the car to ride and handle well.

SPRING TERMS WORTH KNOWING

Free height: A coil spring's free height is measured with the spring out of the car. The free height is the height of a spring when it is unloaded, or not supporting any weight. A spring installed in a car is slightly compressed, so the free height cannot be measured in place.

Spring weight: This is the amount of weight required to compress a spring to a predetermined dimension. The term generally is used in reference to coil springs.

Deflection rate: The deflection rate of a spring is the amount a spring will bend under the influence of a specific weight. Deflection rate of a spring usually is expressed in pounds per inch (pound of weight applied per inch of deflection). For example, if 100 pounds of weight would deflect a spring 1 inch, each additional 100 pounds would result in another inch of deflection. This term usually refers to leaf springs.

Elastic limit: This is the greatest amount of weight a spring can handle and still resume its original height when the weight is removed. If a spring is loaded beyond its elastic limit, it will become permanently deformed or damaged.

Frequency: This term refers to the number of bounces, or oscillations per minute, a spring produces when it is actuated by a bump or dip. The rate is constant for any given spring. Frequency is determined by length, breadth, and thickness.

Sprung weight: This term refers to the weight of everything on the car supported by the springs. Unsprung weight, on the other hand, is the total weight of all parts not supported by the springs, such as axles, hubs, etc. Unsprung weight usually is kept as low as possible in relation to sprung weight because the greater the unsprung weight of a car, the rougher its ride. High unsprung weight is why a pickup truck's ride is so choppy when it is not carrying a load.

Shackles: These are the steel straps that attach leaf springs to frames. Shackles allow a leaf spring to flatten and pivot under load. Pivot points at shackle ends are a common source of problems.

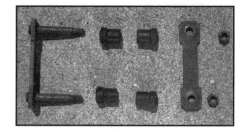

This is a typical shackle replacement kit that uses rubber bushings. Never lube rubber parts with petroleum products.

To remove ball joints, a pickle fork such as the one shown here is needed. It should be placed between the ball joint and the lower control arm and struck with a hammer to free the joint. Or use the more gentle approach with the Tie Rod Puller from Eastwood.

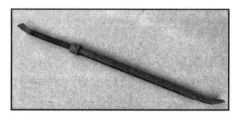

Spring extenders are wedged under the eyes of leaf springs to hold them during removal. They also spread springs for installation.

for your vehicle, such as which engine it has, whether it has an automatic transmission, whether it was set up for commercial use (police car, taxi, or hearse), and whether it has accessories such as the dual side-mounted spare tires common on '30s cars.

One source of springs and suspension parts for most cars is Kanter Auto Products in New Jersey. Contact them at:

Kanter Auto Products
76 Monroe St.
Boonton, NJ 07005

Orders telephone:
(800) 526-1096

Information telephone:
(201) 334-9575

Another good source I have used and recommend is:

Valley Spring
875 Cotting St., Unit L
Vacaville, CA 95688
Phone (707) 449-1929

INSTALLING NEW SPRINGS

On most cars it doesn't matter, but on a few there are left and right springs. Don't mix them up. On some cars, spring ends must be properly oriented in their mounts. Check your car's shop manual for information. Also, it's a good idea to compare the new springs to the old ones to make sure they are the same thickness, have the same number of coils, and are the same

diameter. If any of these dimensions are wrong, send the new springs back and request correct ones. Finally, check the free height of your new springs to make sure they match the figure in your shop manual. You won't be able to compare new springs to the old ones in order to check free height because the old ones will be fatigued.

To install your new springs, use spring compressors to clamp the spring so it will fit in its mounts. Now jack the lower control arm back into place and attach the ball joint or install the pin. Reattach the stabilizer bar, then reinstall the shock absorber.

FRONT END OF CAR IS TOO LOW

Unless your tires are underinflated, this is a sure sign of fatigued springs. You can verify if your car's front springs have sagged by measuring from the bottom of the frame to the top of the lower control arm, then checking this dimension with the specification in your shop manual. If the dimension on your car is an inch smaller than specs, you will need to replace the front coil springs. If you have installed a bigger, heavier engine in a car that originally had a small, light engine, original springs will not be stout enough to keep the front end level.

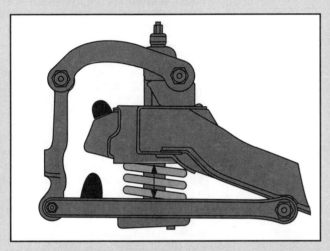

Determine whether your front springs are sagging by measuring from the top of the lower A arm to the bottom of the frame and comparing this figure with specs in the shop manual.

REAR END OF CAR IS TOO LOW

Usually, if your car's back end droops, it's because the rear springs are tired. (If you have new springs in the front of your car that are too stiff, causing it to sit too high, the back end will of course look too low.) Determine whether the rear springs are sagging by measuring from the bottom of the frame to the top of the axle along its centerline.

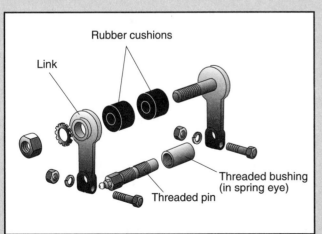

Link

Rubber cushions

Threaded bushing (in spring eye)

Threaded pin

This is how a '60s-era Mustang shackle is constructed.

If the dimension is smaller than the one specified in your shop manual, replace the springs. (Leaf springs can be removed and re-arched, but the results will likely be temporary.) Replace rear coil springs if they are sagging.

CAR SAGS AT ONE CORNER

If one spring is fatigued or broken, it will cause the car to droop to one side. If this is the problem with your vehicle, replace the one on the other side of the car as well as the broken spring. Always replace springs in pairs. If you replace only one spring, your suspension will be fighting itself and you will be the one who loses because the car will ride and handle badly.

CAR HAS A HARSH RIDE

Sometimes, if there are grease fittings on the shackles, a little grease will solve your problem. Or the problem may be caused by dirty, rusted rear leaf springs. You can easily fix this problem by removing, cleaning, and repairing the springs. The shackle pins and bushings will probably need attention, too.

CAR IS HARD TO STEER

This could be caused by a number of things, such as low or uneven tire pressure, excessive caster, or a steering gear that is adjusted too tight. But it might also be a result of weak, sagging front springs. Check the measurements as outlined above. If the dimension on either or both sides is less than specified, replace the springs.

ERRATIC STEERING WHEN BRAKES ARE APPLIED

This would most likely be a brake problem, such as fluid or oil on the brake linings, but it could be insufficient caster in the front wheels. Another possibility is a bent steering knuckle, or it may be a sagging front spring.

CAR PULLS TO ONE SIDE

This could be any of the things mentioned previously, or it could be a tight or dry wheel bearing or a bent frame. The problem could also be sagging front springs or a misalignment of the back axle due to loose mountings at the leaf springs. Carefully measure from a fixed point on the frame to the axle. The distance should be equal on both sides. If it isn't, check a shop manual for the correct dimension, then align the axle and tighten the axle's U bolts to about 65-70 lbs./ft.

ROAD SHOCKS ARE FELT AT THE STEERING WHEEL

This could be the result of having the wrong size or type of tires on the car, or it might be caused by bad or incorrect shock absorbers. It is also possible that your car's front springs have sagged, making them unable to absorb bumps.

COIL SPRING REMOVAL

The following set of instructions will work for most cars built during the '50s through '70s, but check your shop manual for details peculiar to your car. If your vehicle was made during the late '30s or '40s, it probably will have its shock absorbers built into the upper control arms. That will necessitate detaching the lower control arm at the center, where it meets the frame rather than at the steering knuckle, as is standard on later cars.

Block the back wheels, set the hand brake, then jack up the front of your chassis and put quality jack stands under its frame. Place the stands at the jack-points if your car has a unitized body. Remove the front wheels. Now remove the shock absorber from the inside of the spring. Usually there is one retaining nut at the top and two or three at the bottom holding the shock in place. When you remove the top nut, use channel locks to keep the shock absorber from turning, or try the Shock Absorber Tool from Eastwood. This neat tool is a socket within a socket that holds the stud. Disconnect the stabilizer bar from the lower control arm.

Next, wrap a strong chain over the top of the spring mounting recess in the frame, then secure the chain with a bolt and nut to the bottom frame of a hydraulic floor jack. The chain secures the car and limits the spring as you pump up the jack, thus compressing the spring. Jack up the lower control arm until the upper control arm clears its rubber rebound bumper.

Remove the ball joint retaining nut if your car has ball joints. To remove the ball joint, tap on the tapered, upper part of the steering knuckle to loosen it. Do not tap the ball joint itself because you could damage the threads. You will need a tool called a pickle fork to get your ball joints out of their sockets. Or, if you plan to reuse the ball joints, use the Tie Rod Puller from Eastwood. This adjustable puller can be used for removing most suspension and steering joints without damage. If your car is an older one with kingpin and bushing type steering knuckles, remove the pin that attaches the knuckle to the lower control arm.

For safety, slip a two-foot, heavy steel rod or sturdy piece of angle iron up through the hole that was occupied by the shock absorber. Now carefully and slowly lower the jack. Coil springs can fly out with considerable force if suddenly released. Use caution as you perform this procedure. When all of the tension is released from the spring, lift it out of its mounts. Remove the rubber insulating pads.

These '30s-era shackles used pins, bronze inserts, and cork seals. If kits aren't available for your make, and yours need replacing, have a machine shop press out the old bronze bushings and press in new.

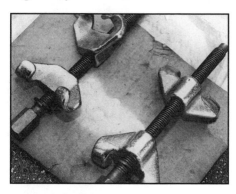

Spring compressors are a must for safe coil-spring installation. Buy them at an auto supply shop or rent them from a tool yard. If you want to do this more than once, check out the variety of spring compressors available from Eastwood.

RUDIMENTARY REPAIRS

Sometimes, with rear leaf springs that are dirty and rusty, the car will ride harshly. You can lubricate them without removing them from the chassis. Clean your springs with a wire brush, then spray them with a graphite or Teflon-type lubricant like Dri-Slide, available at bicycle shops for lubing chains. Heavy Duty Antirust from Eastwood works well, too. Don't use ordinary penetrating oil because you could damage any wax-permeated strips or rubber inserts that may be sandwiched between the spring's leaves. Work the lubricant in by bouncing the car, then shoot on more lubricant until the springs are loosened and the squeaking stops.

Many old car leaf springs have galvanized sheet metal jackets. Under these jackets there is usually a canvas cover. A device used to be marketed that looked like a C clamp with a grease fitting on it that would allow you to shoot grease into a hole in the metal spring cover. If your springs have metal covers, and you can find one of these devices, you are in luck. Drill small holes in the metal spring covers about two-thirds of the way from the center of the spring, attach the clamp, and shoot in the grease. Shoot a drop of silicone seal on the hole to cover it when you are finished. Unfortunately, your chances of finding such a C-clamp device today are slim.

The alternative is to remove the springs from the car, remove the metal covers and canvas, and lubricate your springs.

REMOVING LEAF SPRINGS

Block the front wheels, then jack up the rear of the chassis, placing jack stands under the frame or at the proper jack points if your car has a unitized body. The back axle should be hanging down from the frame, held only by the rear leaf springs. Place your jack under the differential housing and jack up the axle high enough to support its weight. Support the axle on jack stands.

Remove the nuts on the U bolts holding the axle to the springs. Now lift off the U bolts and attaching plates. Using a spring spreader, spread one of the springs until it is in its normal shape. Remove the pins or bolts at the shackles, then remove the spring from the car. Do the same on the other side.

SPRING CLEANING

To thoroughly recondition your car's leaf springs, take them apart and clean any rust and dirt off the leaves. If your springs have sheet metal coverings, they can be carefully removed using a flat chisel and small hammer. Carefully open the seams on the tops of the springs, then pry them off. Remove any canvas jacketing you find. Remove the clips at the ends of the shorter leaves and set them aside. Next, remove the center carriage bolt that holds the spring together. Between the leaves of your springs you may find strips of wax-permeated material. If these are in good shape, try not to damage them. If they are in poor condition, check hobby publications for replacements.

Clean each leaf thoroughly. If your springs do not have the wax-strip inserts, lightly coat each leaf with chassis grease. (Do not use grease with the wax strips, as it will damage them.) You might find rubber, bronze, or plastic inserts at the ends of the leaves. If these inserts are in good shape, continue to use them. If they are in poor condition, replace them with the new Teflon types, available from the sources mentioned above.

To reassemble your springs, install any linings between them, then align the leaves and install the center bolt. Now add the spring clips. Do not over-tighten. If you do, your car will have a harsh ride because the spring leaves will not be able to move properly.

Next, inspect your car's shackles. They may have pins and bronze bushings, or they may have rubber inserts. If the bushings are worn, have them pressed out and replaced at a machine shop. If the rubber mountings have deteriorated or are damaged, they will have to be replaced, too. Never shoot any kind of petroleum-based lubricant on rubber bushings, because it will ruin them.

When you have finished rebuilding your springs, give them a coat or two of the correct chassis paint.

REPLACING REAR SPRINGS

The sources listed earlier can also supply new rear-leaf springs. The same rules apply. Make sure you order the correct springs for your particular make, model, and year of car. While you're at it, order new shackle kits, too. When your new springs arrive, compare them carefully with the old ones to make sure they match. Your new springs will not come with metal covers, regardless of whether your old ones had them. If you are an absolute stickler for authenticity, you can put your old covers on the new springs, but if you aren't a fanatic, leave the covers off. Most modern cars don't have spring covers.

INSTALLING LEAF SPRINGS

Using a spring spreader tool, available at rental yards, spread the spring and attach it at the shackles. Reattach the back axle, making sure it is correctly aligned in relation to the frame. (If it isn't,

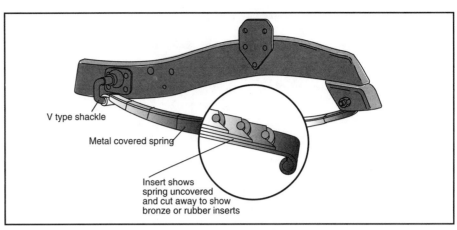

V type shackle

Metal covered spring

Insert shows spring uncovered and cut away to show bronze or rubber inserts

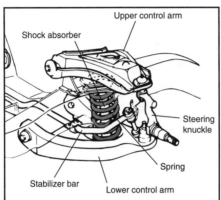

Upper control arm

Shock absorber

Steering knuckle

Spring

Stabilizer bar

Lower control arm

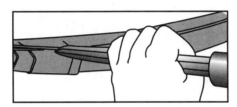

If you need to grease covered springs, remove the metal jackets and canvas covering underneath. If you are a stickler for authenticity, try not to damage the coverings so you can put them back on. If you don't care about total correctness, leave them off.

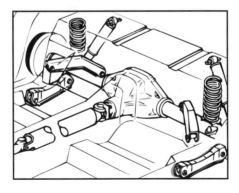

Some cars use coil springs all around. This is a typical late GM setup, but Buick and Oldsmobile were using all coil springs as early as the 1930s.

your car will pull to one side.) Typically, you should tighten the u-bolts to about 50 lbs./ft. of torque, but check a shop manual for the correct spec for your car. Hook up the rear shocks and sway bar.

Some leaf springs have bronze or rubber inserts at the ends of the leaves. These should be replaced when springs are rebuilt.

Late '60s Chevs use ball-joint front suspension. You'll need a pickle fork and a hammer to separate the ball joints. Or, to avoid damage to the grease boot, use the Tie Rod Puller from Eastwood.

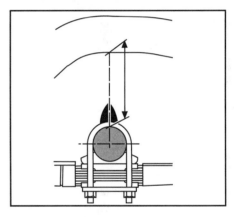

To determine whether rear springs are sagging, measure from the center of the top of the axle to the bottom of the frame and check the figure in the shop manual.

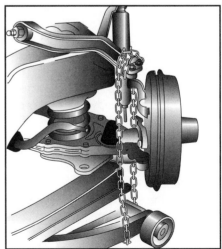

When extricating coil springs, wrap a chain around the upper A arm and the jack before lowering the jack. A coil spring can pop out with a lot of force, causing severe injury.

Engine & Chassis DETAILING
Truck Springs

My old, '58 Chevy pickup had a hard life as a working truck. It was a textbook example of what years of deferred maintenance could do to a vehicle. When I brought it home, its engine was knocking, its rear end was grumbling ominously, and its steering was as sloppy as could be.

Even its springs were sagging and squeaking. It's hard to believe those massive, simple, '50s-era truck suspensions could get tired, but 40 years of hard work takes its toll on the toughest of springs. Chances are if you are the proud owner of an old Apache or F100, or an original '30s-era straight-axle classic, its springs are ready for rehab too if they've never been reworked or have been neglected.

Luckily, the suspension systems on vintage trucks are easy to work on. All that is needed to get your springs out are a few hand tools, a hydraulic jack, and an hour or two of your time. And this recipe will work for any solid-axle classic car or truck.

GETTING THEM OUT

Set the hand brake, block the back wheels, then jack up the front of your truck until the wheels are off the ground. Place sturdy jack stands under its frame. Make sure your truck is steady before climbing under it. Next, place the jack under the front axle and jack it up just enough to take the tension off of the shackles and pivot pins. If your pickup has been badly neglected as mine was, now is a good time to shoot a little grease into the pivot pins so they will come out easily.

Remove the front wheels. Break the nuts loose that hold the shackles in place using two wrenches, then remove the nuts. Pull off the shackles and their rubber grommets. Now place support under the front axle so you can let the axle drop down a few inches. If you don't do this, the axle will flop around on the jack and damage the brake hoses when you loosen the U-bolts.

The shackle pivot pins are threaded into their mounts and should unscrew

easily, but if they are stuck you may have to work them back and forth a bit, or even heat them with a propane torch to get them to move. Once the front shackle pins are out, loosen the nuts and remove the U-bolts. If the nuts are rusted on, use a little WD 40. You can also use heat from a propane torch, plus some judicious tapping with a ball peen hammer to persuade them.

Pull the shock absorbers and their brackets down and out of the way. Pull the U-bolts out, making sure the axle is properly braced. Now roll back on your creeper and loosen the rear pivot pins. Tap them out with a ball peen hammer. If they are badly worn, you may have to push up slightly on the spring eyes to help free the pins. Pull the springs out from under the truck.

Jack up the rear of the truck and put sturdy jack stands under its frame. Remove the rear wheels. Now place your jack under the differential pumpkin and jack up the back axle a little to take the tension off of the shackles and pivots. Slide some supports such as wood blocks under the axle so it can drop down a few inches but not dangle from its brake flex lines. Disassemble the rear shackles the same way you did the front shackles.

Remove the U-bolts and let the spring drop down. Next, remove the nuts holding the keeper pins in place that prevent the front pivot pins from turning. Drive them out using a hammer and drift. Unscrew the pivot pins. You may need to push up on the spring eyes to get the pins free. Pull out the springs.

TROUBLESHOOTING

It's difficult to completely overhaul leaf springs at home. Most of the time on heavy use vehicles they need to be taken apart, inspected for rust and cracks, cleaned, re-arched, and bushed. This kind of work is best left to professionals such as Greg and Tony Meredyk at Vehicle Spring Service in Stanton, California. They do spring overhaul, repair, and replacement on anything from motor homes to off-road vehicles to classic pickups.

My springs were really a mess. The shorter leaves had worn the longer ones down until grooves formed in the longer ones, limiting the spring's flexibility. Also, rust had taken its toll on the leaves, eating away at their strength. Finally, the bushings were elongated and worn to the point of no return. We also had to replace a couple of leaves and clean the others, but since I wanted my truck to sit a little lower, we de-arched the springs.

Arching springs requires a special bulldozer press, and is done cold, because heat destroys the temper in springs and causes them to shatter. Each leaf is worked separately by the rebuilder. These are exacting processes that involve making sure the axle pins remain in the same location when the spring is reassembled, and that the shackles aren't pushed around to an angle where they will be ineffective in the case of de-arching.

Another critical factor with leaf springs is the clips that hold the leaves together. They need to be placed so they don't restrict the spring's flexing action, and they must not be so tight that they bind. Their

It's hard to believe that a system as rugged as a classic pickup's leaf springs could wear out, but they do. At the top of the photo is a broken leaf caused by fatigue. In the middle is a leaf with rust deterioration which causes serious weakening. Near the bottom is a leaf with a groove caused by extensive wear.

Shoot a little grease into front pivot pins to loosen them before removing shackles.

With the front axle properly braced, loosen the U-bolt nuts and remove the bolts. Pull the shock absorbers down and out of the way.

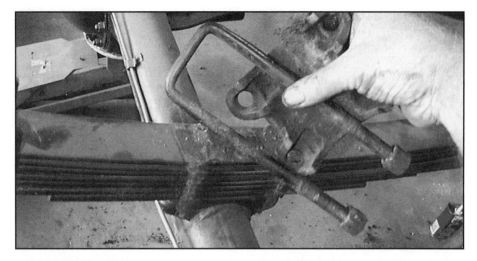

Save brackets, shims, etc. and don't mix them up. The shims at the front axle are to establish caster.

Make sure axles are properly supported so they won't dangle from brake hoses and damage them.

main job is to keep the leaves from fanning over a bump causing the main leaf to take too much of the shock.

INSTALLATION

To put your leaf springs back in, you only need to reverse the steps for taking them out. Just make sure the axle is seated on its locator pin, that the brackets are properly aligned, the caster shims are set in place correctly, and that the pivot pins are properly greased. Also, use only new lock washers where required, and be sure to use only new U-bolts and nuts. Using old U-bolts is courting disaster because if they break, you could loose control of your truck.

Be sure to torque the U-bolt nuts tight. Follow the specs in your shop manual and take them down evenly. Then after you have driven the vehicle for 500 to 1,000 miles, torque the U-bolts again. If you neglect this step, one of the axles could be knocked

askew by a bump and mess up your alignment.

Now when you take your classic out for a cruise, you'll be riding in comfort, because your truck's handling and ride will be all it can be.

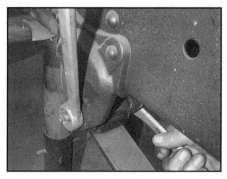

Loosen rear pivot pins of front springs using two wrenches. You may need to push up on the spring eye to free the pin if it is badly worn.

This is the pivot pin from the author's old hauler. No grease and years of hard work have taken their toll. A new pin is at top.

Loosen its nut, then drive out keeper pin for rear spring pivot using a hammer and drift.

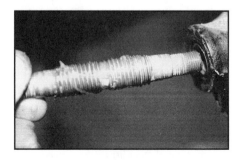

Shackle pivot pins are threaded and should come out easily, but if they have been neglected and are stuck, a little WD 40 and heat from a propane torch may help.

As we said earlier, the suspension systems on vintage haulers are very simple. But that doesn't mean they are unsophisticated. Alignment, toe in, caster, and camber are as critical to steering and handling as they are with any other type of suspension. Maybe even more so, because solid-axle front ends can suffer from wheel tramping and bump steer.

Wheel tramping is when one front wheel bounces up over a bump, telegraphing downward stress along the axle to the opposite wheel causing it to bounce, which then causes the original wheel to bounce again . . . you get the picture. The wheels look like they are high-stepping through something unpleasant. In extreme cases, this can make you lose control of your truck. Wheel tramping is minimized by proper alignment, correct tire balance, and correct shock absorbers.

Another, more common problem with solid axle front ends is bump steer. This happens when one wheel is deflected by a bump, causing the stress to be telegraphed across the tie rod to the opposite wheel deflecting it, and so forth. A vicious shimmy sets in that can only be stopped by accelerating or decelerating. This is a nasty situation that can make you lose control of your truck in a hurry. Bump steer and shimmying can be caused by worn king pins and steering linkage, or more to the point here, by changing the angle of the drag link to something other than parallel to the length of the frame.

If the drag link from the pitman arm of the steering box to the steering knuckle attached to the front wheel is straight and level, the energy from a bump is transferred straight back on the drag link and absorbed. However, if the drag link is angled up or down, it will allow the front wheels to turn when they hit a bump, and it will transfer the resulting energy to the steering wheel and jerk it right out of your hand.

So what does all this have to do with getting your truck to sit a little lower? Just this: If you lower your truck too far or don't pay attention to other components in your front end, you can really mess up its handling. Solid-axle trucks that have been slammed too low will have big problems with bump steer because the drag link will be at a bad angle.

Slammed classics look oh so cool.

Another problem that can occur is for the tie rod ends to hang up on the frame while cornering due to decreased clearance. Also, if you change the ride height of your truck and don't change the shocks to accommodate it, you could end up with serious wheel tramp problems.

Those are the possible pitfalls of lowering, now let's talk technique. The worst way to lower any vehicle is to heat the springs in one spot until they sag. I was surprised to find out that this ancient low-buck slamming technique is still being practiced, dangerous as it is. When you heat a spring, you ruin its temper and make it rigid, brittle, and fragile. The result is a vehicle that is a potential disaster going somewhere to happen.

A better way to slam your classic is to reverse the eyes on the main (longest) leaf. This will net you about 1 1/2" and make your ride look a little sleeker. If you want to drop it more than that, the best way is to de-arch the springs. You can go a maximum of 3" without big problems with bump steer and tie rod clearance.

De-arching is done cold and requires the services of a spring shop such as Vehicle Spring Service. Just as with re-arching, the job has to be done carefully so the axle still sits in the right place and is square to the frame. Never try to heat and de-arch the leaves of your springs at home. This is almost as bad as heating them in one spot, as it destroys the spring.

Other methods that can be used to drop the front end of your truck are lowering blocks or a dropped axle. A dropped axle will work very well if you can find one, but lowering blocks have their drawbacks. Because of the longer U-bolts required and because the axle is further away from the spring, torsional stresses on the springs are increased. For that reason, they are less satisfactory than de-arching.

People have been known to take leaves out of their springs to lower their trucks, but this isn't a good idea either because it puts increased stress on the main leaf, and it messes up the ride of the truck. Besides, it really limits your truck's load carrying capacity. Whatever method you use to slam your truck, you will need to change out its shocks. See the chapter on shock absorbers for more on how to do it correctly.

When you get through installing your de-arched springs, make sure the drag link is parallel to the floor and frame, and that the tie rod ends don't hang up on anything. The pitman arm can be heated and bent a little if need be to correct for the angle. Also make sure your brake hoses aren't kinked. Finally, after slamming it, take your truck in and have the front end realigned to make sure everything is right.

This spring has been heated in one spot to make it sag and lower a truck. Don't try this method. It ruins the spring, spoils your ride, and is dangerous.

This is what a 3" drop looks like. Note that tie rod is close to frame, and there is only about two inches clearance from rubber stubber. Any lower and clearance problems would occur.

Drag link must be parallel to the frame from front to back to avoid bump steer.

Engine & Chassis DETAILING
Shock Absorbers

Bruce Dunbridge, my high school pal, acquired his first car in 1960. It was a 1948 Oldsmobile Dynamic 78 club sedan with a 257-cubic inch flathead, inline eight coupled to a Hydra-Matic transmission. What a machine! It was as big as a locomotive and twice as heavy. Its GM fastback styling, long hood, and pontoon fenders gave it a sleek look. We decided to celebrate Bruce's new-found mobility by inviting our girlfriends to take a spin with us from L.A. to Laguna Beach to have dinner and a walk on the beach. They gleefully accepted.

The big Olds was no longer stylish by the '60s, but it was smooth and silent, and its AM radio worked. We tuned it to the "Mighty 690" (a station out of Tijuana, Mexico, that broadcast with enough power to microwave everybody within 50 miles of its transmitter, playing music our parents loathed). We settled in together for a pleasant drive. The sun was just going down over the Pacific. Don Julian and the Meadowlarks were crooning, "I Can't Get Over You."

Everything pointed to a perfect evening. But it was not to be.

You see, the shock absorbers in the Olds were shot. To make matters worse, the car had coil springs at all four corners. In those days, the coast highway was two lanes of concrete with seams in it about every 50 feet, so Bruce's car began undulating. After each bump, the hood of the Olds rose above the horizon, the front wheels hopped briefly, then the front end plunged until the car almost bottomed out. It did this again and again in a slow, rhythmic fashion as we rolled along. Bruce and I thought this was entertaining, but the ladies didn't agree. My girlfriend had a weak stomach. She became nauseous and cranky. Bruce's girlfriend wasn't happy, either. Things went from bad to worse. We turned back. Our romantic intentions were frustrated by worn shock absorbers.

Ruining your love life isn't all bad shock absorbers can do. In extreme cases, they can make your car handle and ride very poorly, causing severe tire wear. The effects of mere-

ly marginal shocks are more subtle, however. Unless the ones on your car are completely shot, you may not know what you are missing. Most classic cars are surprisingly nice to drive when everything is right on them. But because so many of them have had so little attention paid to suspension systems and steering over the years, we forget how good they were when new. It's sad, because most suspension problems are easily fixed. On cars from the '50s and later, changing shocks is quite simple.

The '48 Olds was an exception. Changing its shocks was a pain. On GM cars of the '40s like Bruce's, the front shock absorbers were integral to the upper A arms. To replace them, you had to take the front suspension apart. The back shocks on the Olds were difficult to deal with, too. They bolted to the brake backing plates, so the wheels had to be removed, then the brake drums pulled before you could unbolt the shock absorbers. Nevertheless, shock absorber technology had come a long way by the 1940s.

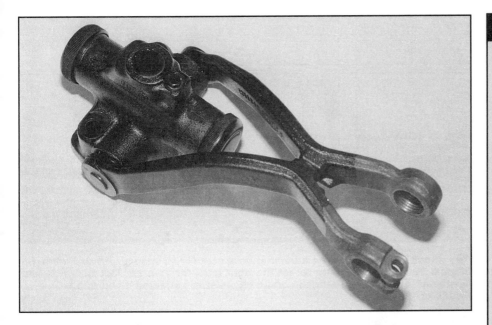

This '40s-era Buick shock absorber is a double-acting lever type that is integrated into the front suspension.

The earliest cars had no shock absorbers at all. Horseless carriages were buggies with gasoline engines. These pioneering autos had gigantic, narrow, spidery wheels so they could roll over potholes without falling into them, and they traveled at very low speeds. They generally had elliptical leaf springs, mounted transversely, both front and rear, to soften the shock of road irregularities. The net effect was that drivers and passengers of such vehicles bounced around like jack-in-the-box puppets when the road got rough.

One of the early devices designed to mitigate this bouncing and bobbing was the Gabriel reel snubber. The snubber had a canvas strap that was attached to the axle and wound into a spring-loaded reel similar in principle to a window blind. It did nothing to damp the initial bounce of the spring, but, to a degree, it slowed and limited rebound. At about the same time, the Truffault friction shock absorber was developed. It used a bronze, cup-shaped shell, a leather disk (or disks) soaked in oil, and a plate (or plates) secured by a bolt that could be tightened to adjust the firmness of the ride. These devices were somewhat better than snubbers, but they didn't hold up well and they didn't work at all when they got hot or wet.

Hydraulic shock absorbers came next and proved to be the best solution to the problem. They were in common use on automobiles by the late '20s. At first, there were single-acting as well as double-acting types. Single-acting hydraulic shock absorbers only slowed the rebound of a spring. Double-acting hydraulic shocks (the types that have been in use since the '30s) dampen spring action on the bounce as well as slow the rebound. They do this by forcing hydraulic fluid through tiny orifices, or valves, as they move. But controlling the action of the springs isn't all shock absorbers do.

They also help control lean in corners and they keep the front end of the car from diving when you hit the brakes. Often, on cars built from the '30s into the early '50s, the shock absorbers were bolted to the anti-sway bars as well as to the springs to keep the car steady on rough roads and in heavy cornering. On brass-era cars, shock absorbers were bolted to the frame of the car and attached to solid axles on both sides of the car, front and rear. It wasn't long before they became much more integrated into the front-end geometry. By the mid-'30s, most cars had independent front suspension with double-acting shock absorbers built into their upper A arms. This design worked very well, but servicing these shocks is more complicated than on cars with the later, direct-acting, aircraft-type tubular shock absorbers.

There are a lot of things that can make an old car ride and handle badly. Shock absorbers are only one factor. Here are some things to check other than shocks:

1) Are tires properly inflated? If tires are overinflated the car will ride hard and its steering will be sensitive. If tires are underinflated, handling will be adversely affected and the car will be hard to steer.

2) Are tires properly balanced and in good shape? Wheel bounce, especially at the front end, is more often due to out-of-balance tires than anything else. Check tires for bubbles, breaks, and other irregularities.

3) Are your car's springs healthy? Many old, front-engine cars have saggy front ends because their springs are tired of carrying all that weight. If the front end sits too low, new shock absorbers won't fix it. Neither will pounding spacers into the springs to get the car level. Spacers will limit spring travel and make the car ride hard. Shock absorbers will be pre-actuated in one direction if the springs sag, so they won't work correctly, either. New springs are the only solution. Rear leaf springs can sag, get stiff, or become noisy in operation. Sometimes all they need is cleaning and lubrication. Check mountings and shackles for problems. If rear springs sag, it is possible to have them re-arched, but the results don't last. New springs are the best answer.

4) Is your steering system all it should be? If your steering box is sloppy due to wear, and if the linkage with the steering knuckles at the wheels is also loose or worn, or if your kingpins and bushings or ball joints need replacing, the car won't steer properly. The front end may shimmy violently and fresh shocks won't help. The front end needs rebuilding.

5) How are the rubber parts? If suspension noise is your problem, check to see that the bottoming stubbers bolted to the frame of your car are supple and that the rubber mountings for the shock absorbers are sound. Also, check the rubber mountings for any links that attach the shock absorbers to the springs or sway bars.

Here is how a typical double-acting '40s era shock absorber looks when disassembled. Parts are difficult to find and specialized tools are required to rebuild them, but there are rebuilders who advertise in hobby publications.

Even tubular shocks come in all shapes and strengths. Be sure to get the right ones for your car, because ride and handling could be adversely affected if you don't.

TROUBLESHOOTING

The simplest way to verify if shock absorbers are working properly is to give them the bounce test. Push down firmly and abruptly on each of your car's front fenders and let them come back up. The car should recover its height, then stop. If it continues to bounce up and down like my buddy Bruce's Olds on that ill-fated night long ago, your shocks aren't working. Perform the same test at the back of the car. It, too, should just return to its old level without bouncing.

If your car won't budge at all when you press on it in the front or back, the valves may be clogged in one or more shock absorbers. If you hear a lot of clinking and clanging, your shocks may be at fault. Let's investigate to see if we can isolate the problem. Most old-style, lever-type shock absorbers used on cars made from the '20s into the late '40s were refilled with fluid on a regular basis.

Shocks from a '60s Mustang are undone at the bottom, then lifted out through the top.

They had a small plug to allow you to do this. If your shocks keep on bouncing, they may need refilling. Many classic-era car manufacturers specified that their shock absorbers be refilled every 10,000 miles, or once a year. If you have a car from this period, obtain some Permatex shock absorber fluid (it's still available, though hard to find) or motorcycle fork fluid to top up the shocks. Some people have used hydraulic-jack oil for this purpose, and it works fairly well, but it does not have the foaming qualities of motorcycle fork fluid. Never use transmission fluid or brake fluid for this application. They will ruin your shocks.

You will need some way to pressure-feed the fluid into the small filler hole in each shock. A squeeze can with a long neck usually will work. Wipe the area around each filler plug clean with a rag and solvent before removing the plug — a tiny bit of grit can ruin a hydraulic shock if it gets inside. Fill each shock until just below the filler hole, then work the car up and down to force out any bubbles. If you can easily disconnect the shock absorber lever to move it up and down in its full range, so much the better for forcing fluid in and air out.

If filling your shocks with the proper fluid seems to help your problem, drive the car for a while, then check for leaks. To do so, run your finger around the seals at the lever-arm pivot points to check for wetness. If you can detach the shock absorber lever, try moving it up and down. It

should require firm, steady pressure through its entire range, although the pressure required will be somewhat less on the downstroke. If you discover any leaks, or your shock offers little or no resistance, they will need to be removed and replaced or rebuilt. And you might as well do all four at the same time, so that they will all function when cornering on uneven roads.

Most later cars with sealed, direct-acting, tubular shock absorbers don't allow for the shocks to be refilled or rebuilt. A few early direct-acting shocks, such as those on Chrysler products of the '30s and '40s can be serviced, but those on cars from the '50s, '60s, and '70s generally cannot. Luckily, replacements are not hard to find for most vehicles. If you are restoring a car for show, try to find the original-type shocks. Good luck. There aren't many left for some cars. But don't despair, because you can paint your replacements the correct color if you can't find originals.

If your shocks need rebuilding, especially if they are the old single-, or double-acting lever types, send them to a place like Five Points Classic Auto Shocks. Five Points has the parts to rebuild anything from old-fashioned canvas snubbers to virtually any kind of lever-type shock, and they have a big stock of hard-to-find, direct-acting tubular shocks. They ship anywhere in the country and usually can return your shocks in 7-10 working days. They also have new links and can supply refill fluid.

Here's the address:

Five Points Classic Auto Shocks
2911A S. Main St.
Santa Ana, CA 92707
phone (714) 979-0451

GETTING THEM OUT OF THE CAR

Getting tubular shock absorbers out of later cars is easy. Jack the car up and put it on good jack stands. Slide your jack under one of the front wheels and lift it up enough so its shock absorber is not fully extended. On some cars, the front shocks come out from the bottom, but others come out through the top of the front suspension. In either case, you will most likely need to reach between the coils of the front springs and hold the shock absorber with a pair of channel locks so it won't turn when you are unbolting it.

You may find it easier to use a tool like the Shock Absorber Tool from Eastwood. This socket within a socket grips the slotted stud while the outer jacket grips the nut. A couple of open-end wrenches grip the stud and nut independently to make quick work of this job. Rear tubular shocks are even easier to remove. Jack up each wheel, then undo the shock absorber. Let the wheel down. Do each corner of the car this way. After you have removed all of the shock absorbers, leave the car on the jack stands until you are ready to install replacements.

If you order new shocks through the mail, you will need to tell the supplier the extended length, the fully compressed length, and the types and dimensions of the shock's mountings.

A word of caution: No matter the make or year, your car's suspension was carefully designed by the manufacturer to work a certain way. Don't try to improve on it. You'll probably make the handling and ride worse. Use original equipment or replacements that meet original specs if possible, unless you are building a street rod, in which case you will need to do a little engineering to make aftermarket shocks work right.

Lever-type shock absorbers on '30s and '40s cars are removed the same way as tubulars (using jack stands and lifting each wheel to take the tension off the shock), but getting the front ones off on some cars (GM and Packard products, for example) will mean taking the whole front suspension apart. If you have one of these, study a shop manual for your car to determine how best to disassemble the front end.

Use spring compressors to clamp the springs together so they won't extend so far that they pop out of their mounts when you remove the upper A arms. This is important because coil springs can come loose with considerable force, causing serious injury. Make careful notes as to how and where any spacers were used to align the front-end assembly, and put them back in the same place when you install the new shocks.

Reassembly is done in the reverse order of disassembly. Use new lock washers and tighten all bolts evenly. Inspect your work carefully before letting the car off the jacks. In cases where the shock absorbers were part of the front-end assembly, you may

Mid-'50s Chev shocks come out through the bottom.

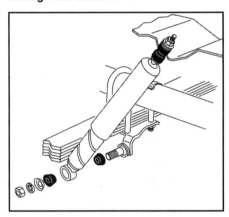

Rear shocks on Mid-'50s Chevs come out from the bottom. Have a friend hold the shock with pipe pliers so you can loosen the upper nut, or use the Shock Absorber Tool from Eastwood.

have to have the front end aligned when you are finished. Finally, don't forget to top up the shocks with the proper fluid every 10,000 miles if they are the old, lever type.

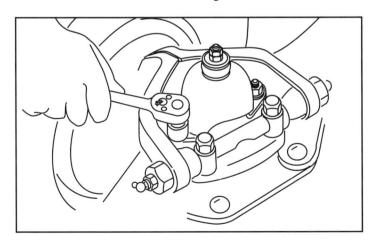

Early '50s Pontiac shocks come out through the top of the chassis. Detach from the bottom first.

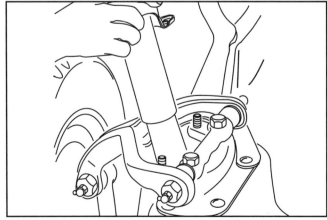

Loosen the support, then lift out the assembly.

Engine & Chassis DETAILING
Steering Boxes

Some years ago, while driving my '38 LaSalle coupe, I remember one extraordinary right turn. When I straightened out the steering wheel, the car kept turning, swinging into the adjacent lane. Horns blared. A guy in a new BMW whom I had unintentionally cut off was particularly displeased.

I had only recently purchased the old LaSalle, so I hadn't yet adjusted to its idiosyncrasies. As I learned, in memorable fashion, it needed front-end work. Someone attempted to compensate for the considerable wear in the entire steering system by just adjusting the steering box. Over-adjusted might be a better description. The lash in the worm-and-roller gears of that old Saginaw box was "adjusted" so the gears bound up in the center. I had to jerk the wheel to get past that tight spot.

This little tale illustrates an important point: Until you eliminate other possible causes for your problems, never adjust the steering box to improve handling. Doing so could ruin a good steering box and still may not remedy your situation. When I

tore down the LaSalle's steering box, I discovered the gears were damaged beyond repair. It took me two years to find a replacement for such a rare old car.

Even though a replacement steering box may be available for your classic, a thorough inspection to isolate the problem comes before messing with your old one. If the steering box is the problem, it's probably not a big deal. If the gears aren't ruined, you can easily adjust them. Or, if need be, you can remove and rebuild the box.

At right are some typical problems and solutions common to all older cars.

THINGS TO LOOK FOR

If you've given your chassis a good lube job, properly inflated its tires, and made sure the front end is properly aligned but are still having problems, check each component of your steering assembly and suspension for worn parts before doing anything to the steering box. Jack up your car so the front wheels are off the ground, then put it on sturdy jack

stands. Turn the steering wheel so the front wheels face straight ahead.

Get under the car, then grasp each component of the steering system and try to move it. There should be no slop in the tie rods, connecting arms, kingpins, ball joints, steering knuckles, or pitman arm. If there is, replace the worn parts before attempting to adjust your steering box. Also check for bent tie rods, steering knuckles, steering arms, or a bent pitman arm. Look for signs of a bent frame.

Sometimes you can spot a bent frame easily just by looking. Inspect for crush deformities especially around the frame ends where the bumper brackets bolt in. Also look for bulges or amateur welds along the frame rails. Finally, use a tape measure and see if the frame is the same dimension from the left corner of the front cross brace to the right corner of the rear cross brace and vice versa. If it is more than 1/4 inch out, you have a bent frame.

Make sure the back axle is properly attached to the springs, and that it is

Mark the steering wheel in relation to the column before removing the wheel so you can put it back on oriented properly.

Use a steering wheel puller to remove the wheel from the splined column. Be careful, though, because steering wheels can come off with a lot of force.

correctly aligned. Again, you can verify this by measuring from fixed points on the frame to the back axle mounts. Make sure the front wheel bearings are in good shape (not galled or worn), freshly greased, and adjusted to the correct preload according to your shop manual. Fix any problems before going farther. I once owned a '40 Packard coupe, that before I restored it, shimmied and whined in two-part harmony when you turned left or right due to worn and neglected wheel bearings. The previous owner was lucky he didn't lose a front wheel under the circumstances.

MAKING THE ADJUSTMENT

There have been several different steering-gear systems used over the years, but all are designed to solve the same problems. Light, responsive steering makes a car enjoyable to drive. The gear ratio in the steering box must minimize effort, but not require excessive wheel turns. The steering gear arrangement must also be nonreversable. It should allow the driver to turn the car, but prevent bumps and road shocks from being transmitted back through the

TROUBLESHOOTING STEERING PROBLEMS

HARD STEERING

Possible causes:
1) Underinflated tires.
2) Steering gear or joints not properly lubricated.
3) Excessive caster in front wheels.
4) Suspension arms or steering knuckles bent or twisted.
5) Sagging front springs.
6) Steering gear too tightly adjusted.

Remedies:
1) Inflate tires to specified pressure.
2) Treat the car to a lube job and top-up the steering box with 90-weight standard transmission oil.
3) Have front end aligned.
4) Replace bent part(s).
5) Replace sagging springs.
6) Adjust lash in steering gear.

EXCESSIVE PLAY OR LOOSENESS IN STEERING

Possible causes:
1) Front wheel bearings adjusted too loose or are badly worn.
2) Steering knuckle bearings worn.
3) Steering gear or connections are adjusted too loose or are worn.

Remedies:
1) Adjust bearings or replace them if worn.
2) Replace bearings.
3) Install new parts as necessary or adjust steering gear.

CAR PULLS TO ONE SIDE

Possible causes:
1) Low or uneven tire pressure.
2) Incorrect or uneven caster, camber, or toe-in.
3) Wheel bearings adjusted too tight.
4) Sagging front spring.
5) Oil or brake fluid on brakes.
6) Brakes incorrectly adjusted.
7) Steering knuckle bent.
8) Frame bent due to collision.
9) Shock absorbers inoperative.
10) Tires are of different sizes.

Remedies:
1) Inflate to specifications in driver's manual.
2) Adjust caster, camber, or toe-in.
3) Readjust bearings.
4) Replace springs.
5) Fix leak and replace linings.
6) Readjust brakes.
7) Replace steering knuckle.
8) Straighten frame.
9) Replace shocks.
10) Replace tires with recommended size.

FRONT-WHEEL SHIMMY

Possible causes:
1) Low or uneven tire pressure.
2) Wheels, tires, or brake drums out of balance.
3) Worn kingpins and bushings, or bad wheel bearings.
4) Steering connections worn or incorrectly adjusted.
5) Steering gear incorrectly adjusted.

Remedies:
1) Inflate to specifications.
2) Balance wheels, tires, and drums. Also check tires for bulges.
3) Replace worn parts.
4) Adjust or replace as necessary.
5) Take up slack in steering gear.

CAR WANDERS

Possible causes:
1) Steering knuckle bearings worn.
2) Incorrect front end alignment.
3) Rear axle has shifted.
4) Steering gear or connections adjusted too loose or are worn.
5) Steering gear or connections adjusted too tightly.

Remedies:
1) Replace bearings.
2) Align front end.
3) Check spring clips for looseness. Measure from rear-spring bolt to housing. The distance should be equal on both sides of car.
4) Adjust or replace gears and bearings in steering box.
5) Adjust properly.

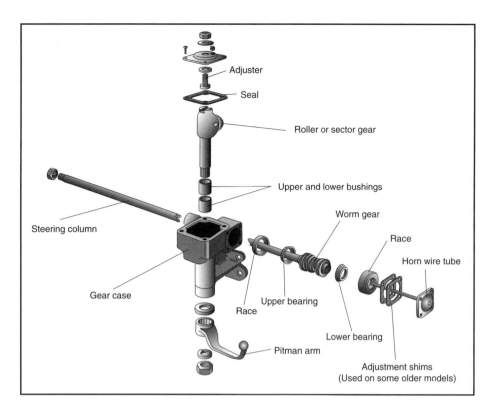

This is an exploded view of a typical worm-and-roller steering box. There are three basic types of steering boxes in older cars, and many slight variations on each of them, but the basic adjustments are similar.

system, deflecting the steering wheel. The three most common designs installed by various car manufacturers are the worm-and-sector (or roller) type, the recirculating-ball type, and the cam-and-lever type.

Power steering systems sometimes have the actuating mechanisms integrated into the steering box, but adjusting the box is done essentially the same way as described below. As with any set of general instructions though, it is best to also check your shop manual for specifics.

For years, Gemmer made the majority of the worm-and-sector steering boxes for American cars. Gemmer steering boxes were used from the '30s into the '50s on Chrysler's line as well as Ford products, and they appear on Packards

and Nashes, too. Their design uses an hour-glass shaped worm gear at the end of the steering column to turn a sector gear on the cross-shaft (also called the pitman-arm shaft or sector shaft) that in turn actuates the pitman arm. The exploded view illustration shows the construction of a typical Gemmer steering box.

General Motors used Saginaw steering boxes. Some were simple worm-and-roller types, but others-such as those used on '30s, '40s, and '50s and later Cadillacs, Chevys, and some Ford products were a recirculating-ball design. The recirculating ball steering box had a special sliding nut that rode the worm gear on loose ball bearings that circulated and were fed back to the beginning by tubes on the outside of the nut. The nut then drove a sector gear that moved the pitman arm shaft. Because ball bearings roll with almost no friction, steering effort was minimized with this innovation.

A third steering box type was the Ross cam-and-lever design. Studebaker used these. A cam attached to the cross shaft had one or two pins that rode up and down the worm gear's grooves, thus actuating the pitman arm. This design resulted in smooth, comfortable steering because it eliminated "rebound" over bumps.

These designs are adjusted somewhat differently, but in each case, the desired outcome is the same. The pitman arm needs to be lined up along the length of the car, the steering gears should be correctly aligned so the wheels are straight ahead and the steering wheel is centered, and the lash between the gears must be correct. Also, there should be no endplay in the sector shaft or steering column. Here's how to check and adjust them.

The adjustment process for the worm-and-sector or roller-type box (our chosen example), is similar to the process used on other steering boxes as well, even into the '70s and '80s. Over the years, steering-box design has improved in many minor ways, though, so check a shop manual or Chilton's Guide to see how your car's steering box is configured before attempting adjustment.

Jack up the car so the front wheels are off the ground, then put the car on

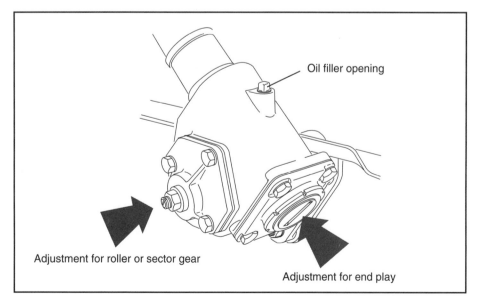

On mid-'50s Chevys, the pitman arm shaft and worm gear end-play can be adjusted without removing shims. On many other cars, shims need to be removed from under the access plate.

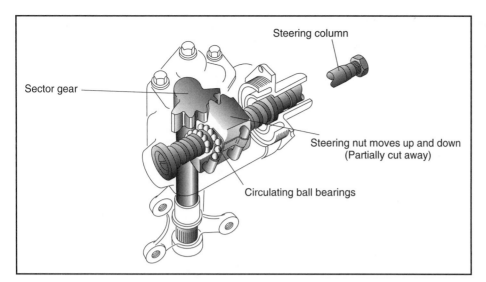

The worm gear bearings and races should be checked for wear and pitting. If bearings aren't clean and shiny or don't turn freely in their cups, replace them.

This is how a circulating ball steering box works.

If sector gear shaft bushings are worn, new ones will need to be pressed in at a machine shop, then burnished to the correct clearance.

jack stands. Roll under the car and disconnect the steering connecting arm from the pitman arm. Do this by removing the cotter key in its end, then unscrewing the plug behind the key. Count the number of turns it takes to unscrew the plug and note it so you can reinstall it with the same spring tension. Finally, make sure the bolts holding the steering box to the frame are tight.

Get inside the car and loosen the steering-column mounting bracket to relieve any tension on the column. If the column is sprung while you are working due to hitting curbs or other misalignment problems, your adjustment will be adversely affected. After adjusting the steering box, if you discover that the column is in poor alignment, use shims, or elongate the steering-bracket mounting holes, to relieve the stress.

ADJUST THE SECTOR SHAFT END-PLAY

Next, turn the steering wheel all the way in either direction until it stops, then turn it back 1/8 turn. The hourglass worm gear in a worm-and-roller steering box is made in such a way that it allows more gap between it and the sector gear at its extreme ends and less in the middle. So when you turn the wheel until it stops, then back slightly, there will be enough tolerance between the two gears to enable you to accurately check the sector gear (or roller) end-play without interference from the worm gear.

On the top of the steering box is an adjuster screw with a lock nut. Loosen the lock nut, tighten the adjuster screw until it's snug, then back it off until it is free. Finally, tighten the adjuster screw slowly until you feel it just touch the top of the sector shaft. Hold it from turning while you tighten the lock nut.

Next, get underneath and check the sector shaft end-play by attempting to move the shaft up and down. If there is still end-play, readjust and test it again. If end-play problems persist after a second adjustment, you may be able to remedy the matter (depending on the design of your steering box) by removing shims from under the plate on top of the steering box. Otherwise, you need to rebuild the box.

The next adjustment is to eliminate steering column end-play. Turn the steering all the way right or left, then back off 1/8 turn. Get in the car and try to pull the steering wheel up and push it down. If there is any movement, it indicates excessive end-play. On steering boxes from the '30s and '40s, adjusting for end-play is a little more trouble than on later cars, because it requires you to loosen the end plate against which the worm gear rides, then remove shims to compensate for wear.

If your car has one of these early boxes, put a pan under the end plate to catch the drippings. Then loosen it evenly and gently pull back on it until its gaskets and shims separate from the main steering box casing. If it doesn't come apart easily, use a sharp putty knife to work it loose, but be careful not to ruin any of the thin metal shims or the gaskets. There should be three or four shims. Just pull out one thin shim and tighten things back up and test the end play. If there are no shims left, the end play is all adjusted out.

A more accurate way to test whether the end-play is where it should be is with a small, spring-type weighing scale available at bait and tackle shops. Fishermen use them to weigh their catches. Attach one hook of the scale on a spoke of the steering wheel and tug gently. Generally, the lash is about right when the pull on the scale required to move the wheel is between 1-1/2 and 2-1/2 pounds. If the pull is lighter, remove another shim. If heavier, add a shim. If you only removed one thin shim to begin with, your steering shouldn't be so stiff that you need to add a shim to loosen it.

More recent steering boxes from the mid-'50s and later allow end-play adjustment between the worm and

REBUILDING

To rebuild your steering box, remove it from the car. On early cars with floor shifts, the job is easy. On cars of the '50s and later it's a little more complicated. It involves removing the decorative panels around the column inside the car and disconnecting the shift linkage. Check the shop manual for your car to determine the best way to do this. Finally, loosen the steering column bracket and remove it.

To get the steering column and box out, you will also need to remove the steering wheel. Many tool-rental businesses have a steering-wheel puller, or you can buy one. Before you start pulling the wheel, disconnect the horn wire at the base of the steering box. Attach a 4-foot length of sturdy string to it.

Next, remove the horn button. Often you can remove the horn button by pressing it in, then turning it a quarter turn. (Some '50s and '60s horn button assemblies come loose by detaching screws from behind.) Usually, the horn wire is attached to the horn button. Pull the horn button up so the wire comes up and out of the tube. Untie the string. (The reason for the string is so you can thread the horn wire back down through the column and box and out the bottom when you put the steering box back in.) Remove the horn contact ring and spring.

Mark the steering wheel and steering shaft with a punch or small scribe so you will be able to align the steering wheel when you put it back on. Attach the steering wheel puller and slowly tighten it, but be prepared. Steering wheels can come off with a lot of force and give you an upper cut you won't soon forget. Remove the spring and small bearing at the top of the steering column jacket.

Get under the car and disconnect the steering connecting-arm as outlined in the adjustment section. Next, with a small chisel, mark the pitman arm and cross shaft so you will be able to put the pitman arm back on correctly during reassembly. Remove the pitman arm. A small gear puller will usually do the job, or you can use one of those wedge-shaped pickle bars made

for separating ball joints. Eastwood sells a purpose-made pitman Arm Puller. This heavy-duty tool applies pressure evenly so as to avoid damage.

Remove the splash pan that goes between the frame and the engine if there is one, and put its screws back in their holes so they won't get lost. Unbolt the steering box from the frame of the car. The steering column and box can now be pulled down and out. (You may have to jack the front end of the car a little higher than usual for it to clear).

Scrape off any caked grime on the box, then wash it down with solvent. You won't want any dirt getting into the bearings and bushings when you open the steering box. When you've got everything clean, grip the box in a vise by one of its bolt pads so it is approximately level. Remove the steering column jacket tube and its clamp.

Next, remove the plate that covers the pitman arm shaft on top of the steering box casing. Save its gasket so you can cut a new one later. Wrap the splined end of the sector gear shaft with electrical tape to prevent damage to the seal in the casing. Now lift the sector gear shaft out the top of the box. Remove the end plate from the casing and pull out the bearing cup and lower worm gear bearing. On some makes there will also be an adjusting sleeve that needs to come out.

Lift the sector, or roller gear, out through the top of the case. Pull the worm gear and steering column out through the end of the case. Inspect the worm and the sector or roller gears. If they are chipped, pitted, or badly worn you will need to find a new, or good used set from another box.

The sector gear or roller is integral to the shaft on most designs, so you will need to change out the complete assembly. The worm gear is usually keyed to the steering shaft and can be pressed off using a bearing press, if necessary. If you don't have a bearing press, take the assembly to a local machine shop and have them press it off for you.

Next, look over the worm gear bearings and their cups for pitting and wear. The races should be free

of pitting, discoloration, and galling, and the bearings should turn freely without any catches. The bearings should also be held firmly in their cages. If they aren't, replace both the bearing and its outer cup. In some cases, the inner bearing race on the steering gear is cast integrally with the worm gear. If the races are ruined on your worm gear, you may be able to have the race built up with welding rod, then re-machined and hard-chromed. Hopefully, you'll be able to find a replacement instead of having to go to such expense.

If you need to change the outer bearing cup for the upper worm gear bearing, you will probably need to have a machine shop pull it out of the steering box casing for you. It is usually pressed in, and it is difficult to get at from behind. While you are at the machine shop, have them press in the new bearing cup. Don't be tempted to try to use a new bearing in an old bearing cup. Bearings and races are machined to work as a set for maximum durability.

Check the bushings in the pitman arm shaft housing. If they are worn, pitted, or damaged, you will need to have a machine shop press them out and press in new ones, then burnish them to fit the pitman arm shaft.

REASSEMBLING

Check the steering column seal in the upper end of the steering box casing. If it is damaged or deformed, replace it. Smear a little gear oil on the upper worm gear bearing and slide it onto its race. Carefully slip the steering column back up through the seal in the upper casing. If there is an adjusting sleeve in your steering box, put it in now. Oil, then install the lower worm gear bearing and cup.

Coat the mating surfaces of the worm gear end plate with sealer, then press on a new gasket. If your steering box is an older one that employs shims for adjustment, slip them over the horn wire string now. Thread the horn wire string down through the tube in the worm gear end plate. Now tighten the end plate evenly into place. Oil its bushings, then slip the pitman arm shaft down into the steering box casing until its gear or roller engages the worm gear. Install a new gasket and tighten the cover into place.

Remove the steering wheel again and carefully slide the steering column mast jacket onto the column and tighten its clamp. Put any felt oiling pads in place, then reinstall the upper steering column bearing.

With the steering box still clamped in the vise, temporarily install the steering wheel, then adjust the worm and sector gear lash and end-play according to the instructions in the adjustment section. Install any shift linkage that needs to be added before putting the steering box assembly back in the car.

Bolt the steering box loosely to the frame. Now get inside the car and loosely install the steering bracket. Put the steering wheel temporarily in place and turn the steering wheel all the way to the left until it stops, then all the way to the right. This is to relieve any binding in the system. Now tighten the steering box and column bracket evenly into place making sure that the column is properly aligned.

Put any shift apparatus back on, then install any decorative jacketing around the steering column.

Pull the worm gear and steering column out through the bottom of the steering box, then inspect the upper worm gear bearing and outer race.

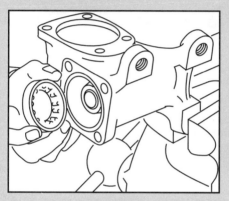

Remove the lower plate, then ease the lower worm gear bearing race out of the casing. Remove the lower worm gear bearing.

Make sure the front wheels are aligned straight ahead. Then, using your reference marks to orient it properly, slide the steering wheel onto its splines. Let the car down off of the jackstands, then tighten down the steering wheel nut.

Slip the horn contact cup, insulator, and spring onto the horn wire. Tie the string hanging out of the steering column to the horn wire, then get out of the car and pull the horn wire down through the column and out through the end plate of the casing. Rotate the horn button into place. Reattach its wire to the feeder wire from the main harness. Fill the steering box with gear lube, then take the car out for a test drive.

If things aren't right, fine tune your adjustments to the steering box. If the steering wheel spokes are not quite lined up, you may have to remove and reinstall the box slightly to the left or right so it lines up properly when the car is going in a straight line. Finally, check your steering box whenever you service the car to make sure it is full of lubricant.

roller by adjusting a sleeve in which the upper roller bearing race of the worm gear is mounted. The adjuster for this sleeve most often is located just below the junction of the steering column and steering box. It usually consists of a lock nut and adjuster screw. As with any type of worm-and-roller steering box, turn the steering wheel all the way in one direction until it stops, then back off 1/8 turn, so there will be plenty of play between the gears before making this adjustment.

After adjusting your steering box, get in the car and turn the steering wheel from one stop to the other. There should be a slightly increased effort required at the center of the turning range. Turn the steering wheel to the middle so the front wheels are pointed straight ahead. Get under the car and see if you can move the pitman arm. If there is any

side-to-side movement, the sector gear adjustment is too loose.

Your fisherman's scale can be used to test for tightness at the high spot at the center. Attach the scale to a steering wheel spoke, out near the rim. Then pull through the high spot. The scale should register no more than 4-1/2 pounds nor less than 3 pounds. If it is less, you need to adjust the gears a little tighter. If more than 4-1/2 pounds of pull is necessary, you need to loosen things a little.

Some worm-and-roller steering boxes have a worm gear end-play adjuster on the lower end of the steering box. It is harder to reach, but the method of adjustment is similar. When you have finished making your adjustments (if disassembly was required), seal the gasket mating-surfaces with silicone sealer, top up the steering box with the same

hypoid gear oil you would use in a standard transmission or differential, then take the car out for a test drive. Your car should steer lightly and smoothly without catches or tight spots. If, after careful adjustment, your steering still isn't right, a rebuild of the steering box may be in order.

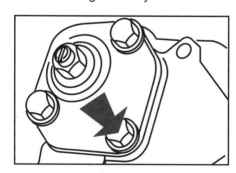

On American Motors cars, as well as on some other makes, you will need to loosen a bolt to replenish the lubricant in the steering box, because no filler opening is provided.

Engine & Chassis DETAILING
Steering Linkage & Suspension

Many restorers believe the front suspension and steering linkage on their classics are too fussy to mess with at home. The truth is, there is nothing to fear. These systems do need to be precisely aligned, but rebuilding and replacing your classic's front end is fairly easy, and with the right tools you can even realign you car's front end yourself. First we'll talk about troubleshooting, then we'll explain how to fix the various problems.

Before beginning your checks, make sure the front wheels are pointed straight ahead so the steering box will be centered, so that there shouldn't be any slack in it, provided it isn't badly worn. Next, make sure the wheel bearings are in good order and properly adjusted.

The reason for this is because loose or worn wheel bearings can allow a wheel to wobble, deceiving you into thinking a ball joint or bushing is defective. Also, no matter what else you do to your car's front suspension and steering, it won't handle or steer as well as it

should if it has bad, maladjusted, or neglected wheel bearings. See Chapter 15 for details on how to replace, adjust, and maintain wheel bearings.

To check out your classic's front suspension and steering, jack the front end up off the ground, then put sturdy jack stands under the frame so the suspension A (control) arms are free and you can move the wheels easily. Grab each front wheel in turn and try pulling out at the top and pushing in at the bottom, then vice versa. If the wobble is more than a quarter of an inch, one or more components in the steering or front suspension is worn and needs replacing.

Next, grip each wheel front and rear and try to wobble it back and forth. If there is any play, the steering linkage or king pins/ball joints are probably worn. You can further isolate steering problems by grabbing the tie rods, drag links, and such and pushing up on them. They should not move. If they do, replace the tie rod ends. To check for ball

joint problems, use a long two-by-four to pry up from under each wheel; watch the ball joints or king pins and cross pins. You can usually locate the worn item pretty easily.

Of course, if you are doing a total restoration on a high mileage car, you will want to rebuild its front end in any case. The job can be done with hand tools for the most part, and shouldn't take more than a weekend or two to complete. There are a lot of variations even on the two most common basic systems, so read over the shop manual for your make and year before beginning the job.

Also, read the section on removing front springs in the chapter on springs in this book for important safety information. Front coil springs are under compression and can pop out with a lot of force. Make sure you use a safety chain around the spring before any disassembly of the front suspension.

Almost any car ever made will have one of two basic steering systems, those being either the king

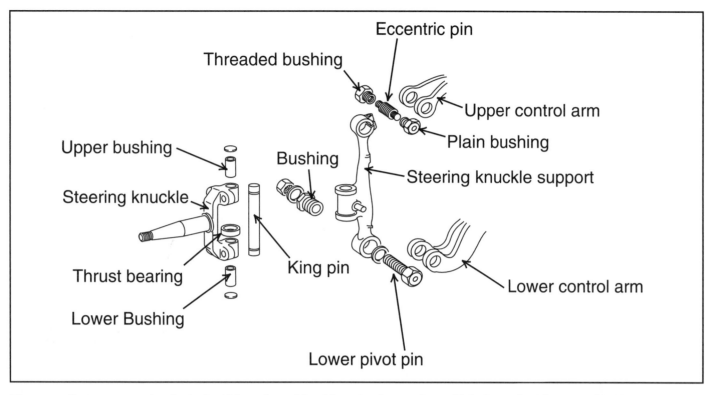

These are the components of a typical king pin and bushing steering system with independent front suspension.

Labels on diagram:
Eccentric pin
Threaded bushing
Upper control arm
Plain bushing
Steering knuckle support
Upper bushing
Bushing
Steering knuckle
King pin
Thrust bearing
Lower Bushing
Lower control arm
Lower pivot pin

pin and bushing type, or the ball joint type. King pin and bushing steering systems were used with the old, solid-axle cars from the beginning, and were retained when unequal length A arm independent suspension came along in the '30s. Some manufacturers, such as Studebaker, continued with king pins and bushings into the '60s. However, most companies had switched to ball joint front suspension by the mid-'50s.

KING PINS

King pins and bushings were a good, rugged solution to the problem, but they didn't allow as tight a turning radius as the later ball joint systems. They were also more expensive to build. If your car has king pins and bushings, there will be a little more involved in rebuilding the system, but it is still no big deal. Here's how:

With the front of the chassis on sturdy jack stands, remove the front wheels by loosening the big wheel bearing nut in the center, then pulling the wheel off, bearings and all. Remove the locking cotter pin. Next, carefully remove the bolts holding the backing plate onto the

steering knuckle. If your brakes are in good condition, leave the shoes in place, and tie the backing plates up out of the way so there is no strain placed on the brake hoses.

Next, wipe the spindles completely clean, then use a Spotcheck Jr. kit, to check them for cracks. Inspect the bases of the spindles especially carefully. A fatigue crack in a spindle could cause the loss of a wheel, and a very serious accident could occur. If you find any problems, have the steering knuckles Magnaflux tested at a local machine shop to confirm your findings, and replace both spindles if you find one that is cracked.

Drive the retainer pins for the king pins out of the steering knuckles using a brass drift, then pry out the expansion caps in the tops of the steering knuckle supports. I usually drive a screwdriver into the cap, then pop it up. Now, depending on how your car is designed, you will need to pop out the lower retainers, or drive the lower bushing up and out using a hammer and drift in the case of a bushing with an enclosed end.

King pin replacement kits are available for most cars, and they usually come with exact size bush-

King pin and bushing steering systems and solid front axles were used from the beginning, and continue to this day on trucks. When bushings are worn, steering becomes sloppy.

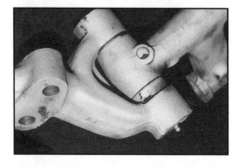

Horizontal pins and bushings like this were sometimes used when king pin and bushing steering was incorporated into independent front suspension.

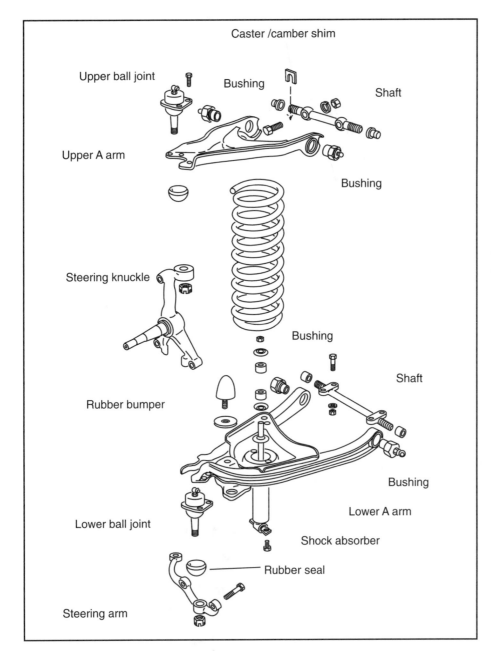

Caster /camber shim

Upper ball joint

Bushing

Shaft

Upper A arm

Bushing

Steering knuckle

Bushing

Rubber bumper

Shaft

Bushing

Lower A arm

Lower ball joint

Shock absorber

Rubber seal

Steering arm

Here is what a typical ball joint steering and front suspension system looks like.

Crusty, worn, neglected ball joints like this will cause your classic to handle badly, and can cause rapid tire wear. Luckily, they are not difficult to replace.

Cars made from the mid-'50s on generally came with ball joint front suspension and steering. They are simpler to replace and allow a tighter turning radius than king pins and bushings.

ings to make the job easy. There are a few cars where the bushings will need to be pressed in, then reamed to the correct size by a machinist. The easiest way to get the old bushings out and the new bushings in is to take them to your local machine shop and have the old ones pressed out and the new ones installed. If the front end isn't too badly worn, this is a simple task, but sometimes the new bushings fall right out because the steering knuckle is also badly worn. In that case, the steering knuckle will have to be reamed out and sleeved back to its correct dimension. Bushings must fit tightly for the repair to be effective.

BALL JOINTS

If one ball joint is bad on your car the others won't be far behind. Replace them all. Generally, ball joints are bolted or riveted into place on the control arms. If yours are riveted into place, drill out the rivet heads and drive the rivets out. Ball joints can be a bit difficult to extricate from the control arm if you don't have a ball joint removal tool. In any case, first remove the self locking nut on top of the joint.

A pickle fork can be tapped into place to separate the joint from the steering knuckle, but never tap on the threaded end with a hammer.

You will distort and ruin the joint. A special tool for the job is available from the Eastwood Company that grips the steering knuckle and forces the ball joint out quite easily. The tool is also ideal for removing tie rod ends.

If you are not sure whether your ball joints need replacing, wipe them off and inspect them carefully for wear. Don't submerge them in cleaning solvent or kerosene

Biodegradable rubber bushings deteriorate with time, even if a car has been in storage. They get hard and brittle and seriously affect ride.

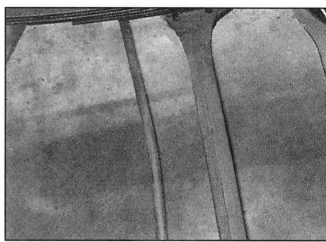

Bent tie rods like this one on a '50s-era pickup mean squirrelly handling and rapid tire wear. Replace linkages like this with straight ones.

though, because doing so will make them impossible to lubricate properly. And don't try to install your new or old ball joints using rivets. It is not possible for a restorer working at home to do it properly. Instead, use the bolts and nuts that come with the replacement ball joints, or get heat-treated bolts from the hardware store.

RUBBER BUSHINGS

The rubber bushings common to most suspension systems made in the last 50 years can be pressed out using a vise, and then new ones pressed in. If you have the front end apart, it is probably a good idea to replace them anyway, because rubber deteriorates over the years, whether the car is used a great deal or not. And if you decide to replace your car's rubber bushings, consider the modern, polygraphite types. They'll last a lot longer than rubber and will improve handling. Front end kits with everything necessary are available for most cars made in the last 50 years.

If you replace the rubber bushings in your car's A arms, replace those on the sway bar, too. The sway bar helps control lean when cornering, so it has a big effect on your classic's handling. If you have installed a bigger engine or race tuned the one you have, consider installing a heavy-duty sway bar and polygraphite bushings.

TIE ROD ENDS

If you can move your tie rods around with your hands, your tie rod ends need replacing. Again, a pickle fork can be used to separate tie rod ends from steering arms, but the easier way is with a joint separator. Tie rods are left-hand threaded on one side, and right-hand threaded on the other, making them similar to a turn buckle. If you loosen the clamps securing the tie-rod ends, you can shorten the tie rod by turning it one way, and lengthen it by turning it the other way using channel locks.

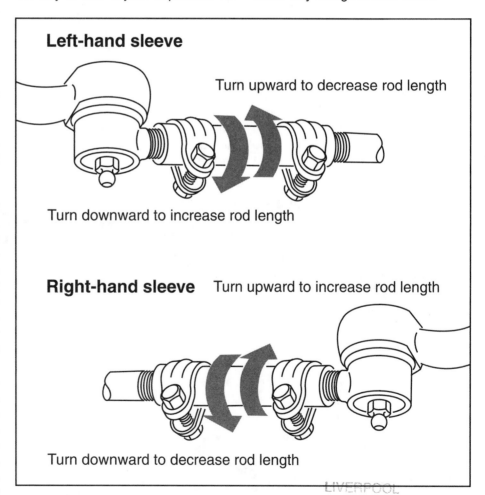

Left-hand sleeve

Turn upward to decrease rod length

Turn downward to increase rod length

Right-hand sleeve   Turn upward to increase rod length

Turn downward to decrease rod length

Tie rods work like turnbuckles. If you turn the rod one way, it shortens and if you turn it the other, it lengthens. Tie rods are right- and left-hand threaded to make this work.

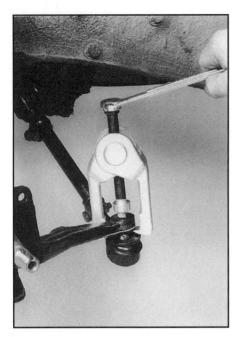

This tie rod puller from the Eastwood Company makes removing ball joints and tie rod ends a snap. Eastwood also sells a Pitman arm puller that is similar and just as effective.

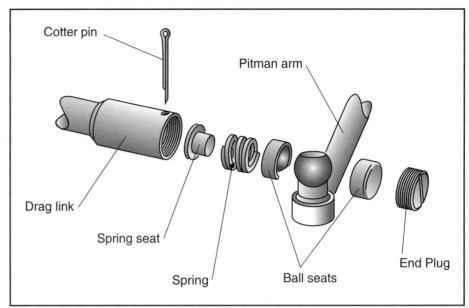

This is a typical drag link and Pitman arm connection. Be sure to count the number of turns required to disassemble it so you can put it back together correctly.

Always replace bent tie rods with new ones. And any time you replace tie rod ends on old tie rods, measure from bolt to bolt to ascertain length, then make a note of it before unscrewing the tie rods. Also, note the number of turns it takes to remove each tie rod end so you can install the new ones the same way. Changing tie rod length changes the toe in/toe out of your car's front wheels.

PITMAN ARMS AND DRAG LINKS

Some earlier steering systems use a Pitman arm and drag link setup in the steering linkage. If you are rebuilding your car's steering, it is a good idea to disassemble the end on the drag link and make sure the ball on the Pitman arm is not galled, worn, or pitted. To do this, remove the cotter pin, then unscrew the end with a slotted screwdriver, counting the number of turns it takes to disassemble the item. Replace worn Pitman arms,

their bearings, and the drag link if they are loose and worn.

ADJUSTMENT ITEMS

There are a couple of ways front suspension systems are aligned. The most common uses shims at the mounting points of the upper A arms. These affect camber, which is usually used to tilt the front wheels in slightly at the bottom so the bottom of the wheel is more directly under the ball joint. That way, the wheel bearings don't have to cope with more side load than necessary.

Shims at the attaching bolts in the upper control arms control camber. Be sure to save them and put them back in the same places when overhauling your car's front end.

On some earlier suspension systems, eccentric shims were used to align suspension. Save them and install them the same as they were originally when putting your suspension back together.

Any time you disassemble your car's front end, make careful note of where such shims go and put them back when you are finished so the camber will be correct.

Other, earlier independent suspension systems use eccentrics in the upper control arm for the same purpose. Be sure to install them back in the same place. While it is important to have your car's front end realigned any time you work on it, you will want to be careful so it won't be so far out that it is dangerous to drive to the alignment shop.

When you get your car's front end back together, recheck all the bolts for proper torque, then make sure any cotter keys or keepers have been replaced with new ones before taking the car down off the jack stands. Once the car is on the floor, push down on the front fenders a couple of times to seat the bushings. Have the front end alignment checked, then take your car out for a test drive. It should handle like new.

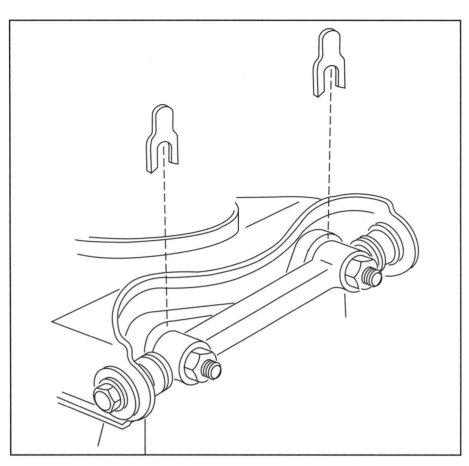

Camber is controlled on most more recent front suspension systems by shims in the upper A arm attachments. Be sure to put them back in the same place when rebuilding your front end.

This lower A arm attachment has been restored to factory fresh, complete with cadmium-plated retainers and cast-iron, spray-coated cross pieces. Not only will the car handle like new but it will look new as well for years to come.

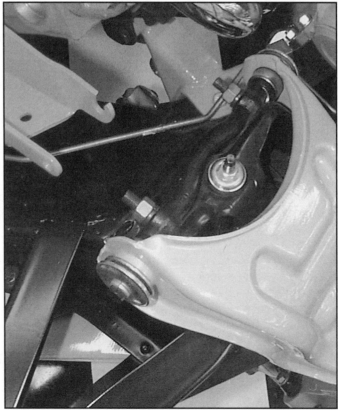

Hot-coated, heavy-duty A arms plus fresh bushings and ball joints mean this Bow Tie street rod will handle well and look good with its hotter engine.

Engine & Chassis DETAILING
Wheel Bearings

There was a loud bang, then a long screech. I looked up to the cross-street, half a block from my house in time to see a '64 Fairlane wheel go rolling by — hubcap and all. I walked to the corner and found the rest of the Fairlane stopped in the middle of the street. It had gouged a 20-foot groove in the asphalt with its passenger-side front suspension. The owner was standing beside his car, dumbfounded. He had no idea what had happened.

I walked up to the wheel where it had come to rest and discovered that a blued and burnt piece of the front spindle was lodged in what was left of the wheel bearings. The hub was still hot. It was obvious that the old Ford's bearings had not seen any grease for a long time. I doubt if the owner even knew that front wheel bearings — as well as rear wheel bearings on some cars — required regular lubrication.

He's not alone. Most people, even old car buffs, don't know

much about wheel bearings. The subject is not usually covered in shop manuals because the task of packing them with grease is considered routine maintenance. Most owner's manuals say wheel bearings need packing every 10,000 miles but don't give a clue how to do it.

Whether you are refurbishing a driver or performing a frame-up restoration, you need to know how to pack or replace front (and possibly rear) wheel bearings. Your life could depend on it. Fortunately, there isn't much to it. The job can be accomplished in a couple of hours using hand tools. Here's how:

Pull on your car's parking brake and jack up the front wheels. Put the car on jack stands. Spread a clean rag newspaper on the floor under one of the front wheels. Pop off the wheel cover, removing the small dust cover in the hub. On most cars, you will find a castillated axle nut held in place by a cotter pin. (Some Chrysler products

from the '50s will have a big nut and a separate locking nut.) Use wire cutters to pull out the cotter pin, then loosen and remove the retaining nut and the slotted washer behind it. Alternatively, use the Cotter Pin Removal Pliers from Eastwood.

Next, jiggle the wheel — tire and all — so the outer wheel bearing falls into your hand. Grab the tire and pull the wheel off, along with the brake drum. (This is easier than first pulling the wheel, then trying to remove the drum and hub afterward.) Try not to drag the inner wheel bearing on the spindle as you pull the wheel off. Lay the wheel on the floor upside down and use a seal puller or a big screwdriver to pop out the inner wheel-bearing seal.

Most cars and trucks made in the last 50 years have either roller or ball front-wheel bearings. Ball bearings, other than being spherical, have a loose, inner race (cone) that comes out separately. But the inner races on roller bearings are integral to the bearings. Either way, packing the bearing is the same.

Turn the wheel over and, using a hardwood dowel or brass drift, drive the inner wheel bearing race out of the hub. Tap evenly around the race so as not to cock it in the hub, which would make it more difficult to remove. Wash out the old bearings in solvent or kerosene, then inspect them carefully. Don't blow them off or spin them with compressed air, because that could damage them. Also, keep the bearings scrupulously clean, since a tiny bit of grit will ruin them in a hurry.

REPACK OR REPLACE?

Are the bearing races shiny and smooth or are they pitted? Do they have a chromelike shine, or are they blued, yellowed, or burned? If they are discolored or pitted, they need replacing. Are the balls or rollers secure in their cages? Also, are balls or rollers smooth and shiny? If not, you need new bearings. If your bearings pass the above tests, shoot a little light oil on them and then turn them slowly in their races. They should roll smoothly, without a hitch or hint of unevenness. If they don't, you need new bearings.

If you need to install new bearings and roller bearings are available, either as original equipment or as replacements, buy the roller types. They are more durable, supporting side loads when cornering better than ball bearings. This could be especially important if you intend to install wider wheels and tires.

Next, clean old grease from the hubs, being careful not to get any of it on brake linings or braking surfaces. Some people pack gobs of extra grease into the hubs thinking it will help the bearings in some way. This is not a good idea because the extra grease holds heat in, then melts, running onto brake linings and causing grabbing and lining damage. The extra grease never gets to the friction surfaces of the bearing anyway, so it does no good and can cause serious damage.

A NOTE OF CAUTION

During assembly, the outer races of the wheel bearings go in first, tapering outward, followed by the bearing, then the inner race if it is loose. Never put a bearing in the other way around (in other words, bearing-and-inner-race first, then the big, outer race, facing in). You could easily lose a wheel.

To install outer bearing races, the easiest way is to use a bearing race and seal installer. Make sure there are no burrs that might stop your bearing race from being pressed into place, then smear a

This seal replacement tool from The Eastwood Company makes wheel bearing work a cinch.

The two types of front-wheel bearings in common use are ball bearings and roller bearings. If you have a choice for your classic, get roller bearings because they are more durable.

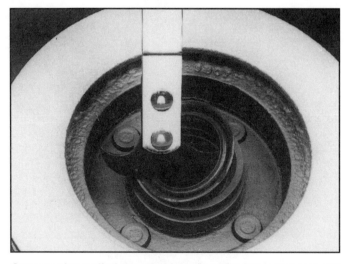

Once you've pulled the wheel, lay it on its back and pop out the rear bearing seal. Use the special tool made for the job or employ a large screwdriver.

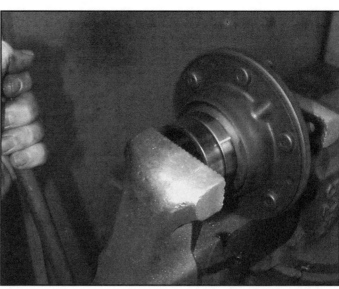

Check wheel bearings for pitting, as shown here, as well as burning and galling. Replace any bearings with these problems.

Bearing races can be pressed in using a bearing and seal-installing tool, a socket of the correct size, or even the old race as a drift.

light coat of oil in the hub. Select the correct drift for the tool, attach the handle, then tap the race into place.

If you don't have a bearing and seal installer, press the races in using a socket of the same diameter, or even the old race as a drift. Gently start the race into the hub by tapping it with a soft hammer, making sure you don't get it cockeyed, then place the socket over the race and use a vise to press the new race into place. If nothing else, tap the race into place using the socket or the old race as a drift. Never hammer directly onto a

race or a bearing because you will ruin it.

Now pack the inner-wheel bearings with grease that is especially designated for the job. Wheel-bearing grease is available for drum as well as disk brakes. Use the correct type for your application. Employ a tool especially made for packing wheel bearings, or use my favorite method: Place a gob of grease on the heel of your hand, then press and drag the back of the bearing into it until you see the grease come up completely around the bearings. Turn the bearing over and press more grease in from the

front. Make sure the bearing is well slathered with grease, then put it into place on its race.

Oil the felt or neoprene seal that rides on the spindle, then tap the seal home using a seal installer or a socket the diameter of the outer rim of the seal. Never try to tap a seal into place directly with a hammer because you will dent and deform it if you do. As a result, grease could run onto your brakes.

Turn the wheel over and install the outer wheel-bearing race. Pack the outer wheel bearing, but don't put it into place until you slide the wheel back onto the spin-

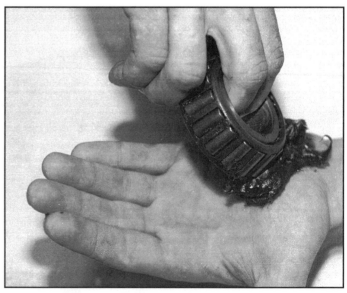

Be sure to install the bearings so their outer races taper away from the center of the hub. To do otherwise could result in a lost wheel.

Grease your bearings using a bearing greaser, or by hand like this. Press and drag the bearing through the grease to force it all the way into the bearing.

Oil the felt or rubber edge of the inner bearing grease seal and line it up on the hub.

Tap the seal into place with a seal installer, an extension, and a socket that is the outer diameter of the seal.

dle. Install the slotted washer, then spin the castillated wheel nut loosely into place.

SETTING THE BEARING PRE-LOAD

Many shop manuals offer a torque specification for wheel bearings. If you find such a spec, use a torque wrench and tighten the castillated nut as specified. For example, a '59 Cadillac's front wheel bearings should be pre-loaded by tightening the castillated nut to 25 foot pounds, then backing off to approximately 4 foot pounds before installing the cotter key.

The usual method if you don't have a torque specification is to use a 10-inch wrench and tighten the wheel nut until the wheel drags noticeably when rotated. Now back off until you can install a new cotter pin, which should be about half a hex, or 1/12 turn. Never loosen the wheel more than that because the bearings need a certain amount of pre-loading. Never use an old cotter pin or one of a smaller size. You could lose a wheel if you do. Finally, install the dust cap on the hub, tighten the lug nuts into place, and install the wheel cover.

Using a 10-inch crescent wrench, tighten the wheel nut until the wheel drags noticeably. Then back off about 1/2 hex so the cotter pin lines up. Install a new cotter pin of the correct size.

PERIODIC PACKING

Some cars, such as '40s-era Chrysler products and Packards until they stopped making them in 1958, require that their rear wheel bearings be packed every 30,000 miles, as well. To do this, take the brake backing plates off. Save any shims you find so you can put them back in place and don't mix them up. Be sure to install a new seal. Tighten the rear axle nuts to the specified torque load (200 lbs./ft. is common). If you don't get the rear axle nuts tight, the axle eventually will strip the drum spline or snap.

Engine & Chassis DETAILING

U-Joints

From the earliest days of the automobile there was the problem of transmitting power from the engine, which is part of a car's sprung weight, to the rear axle, which is part of its unsprung weight. Early designers discovered that springs were needed between the axles and the frame to keep bumps from bashing occupants to bits on rough roads. But they also found that adding the engine and transmission to this sprung weight had a terrible effect on control and riding comfort.

In order to transmit power from the relatively stationary engine mounted in the frame to the up-and-down bouncing rear axle, a number of things were tried. Leather belts, friction rollers, chains, even ropes, were employed. None proved as quiet or as reliable as the Hotchkiss rear axle driven by a driveshaft and coupled by at least one universal joint at the transmission output shaft. Later, two u-joints began to be used, one at the back

of the transmission and one just in front of the differential. Buick, Ford, and Chevrolet used a closed torque tube and shaft with one universal joint up front for many years. Ford went to open drive lines with two u-joints in 1949, and Chev and Buick followed suit in the 1950s.

Cross-and-yoke u-joints with needle bearings were so durable they rarely caused problems — provided they were properly maintained. Unfortunately, they almost never received the necessary attention over the years. On top of that, they were sometimes tortured and abused during jackrabbit starts and panic stops, or by blasting over bumps and railroad tracks at high speed.

Cross-and-yoke universal joints in vintage, open driveline cars need to be packed with grease on a regular basis. (Every 15,000 miles on cars from the 1930s, 25,000 miles on cars from the '50s and '60s.) But because these intervals don't coincide with the regular

lube-and-oil maintenance cycle, u-joints usually were neglected until they caused problems.

On most cars, the only way the u-joints can be serviced is to take them apart, grease them, then put them together again and reinstall them. Some cars have u-joints equipped with grease fittings to make lubrication easier, and many aftermarket u-joints come with a grease nipple. But the person doing the lubricating would sometimes pump grease into them under high pressure, causing their seals to rupture. After that, the joint would fail anyway because of dirt contamination.

If your chassis has an open driveline and u-joints equipped with grease fittings, you are in luck, because they can easily be lubricated using a hand-operated grease gun if they are in good shape. Gently push grease into the fittings, a little at a time. When you feel a slight resistance, stop. If you grease them at the recommended intervals and drive sensi-

Split-yoke u-joints are easiest to install. Make sure you use new locking devices on bolts.

bly, you may never have to change u-joints on your classic.

TROUBLESHOOTING

To inspect u-joints, put the transmission in low gear if it is a standard, or in park if it is an automatic. Jack your car up, placing it on jackstands so all four wheels are off the ground. Now grip the driveshaft and attempt to turn it. If you notice any lash, it is time to replace the u-joints. If you still aren't sure, but suspect your u-joints are worn, take the driveshaft out and see if the joints move smoothly through all of their range of motion. If they are stiff, hang up, or are loose, replace them.

REPLACING U-JOINTS

These instructions are for cars with open driveshafts. For cars equipped with closed, torque-tube drivelines, consult a shop manual to determine how to remove and replace the u-joints. Even on cars with open drivelines, there are several variations on the cross-and-yoke design. There also were the ball-and-trunnion types used as front joints on drive shafts in

'40s-era Chryslers, Dodges, and Plymouths, as well as some Packards.

Kits to overhaul ball-and-trunnion u-joints are available from Mopar clubs. The instructions in Chrysler products shop manuals are clear on how to rebuild these, and the job is pretty simple, so we won't talk further about this rare type of u-joint. Here is what to do with the more common cross-and-yoke type joint:

OUT WITH THE OLD

Get on your creeper, roll to the rear and, using a file or china marker, mark the driveshaft in relation to the rear yoke of the universal joint in order to put the driveshaft back in the way it came out. It

is possible to swap driveshafts end-for-end on some cars, but more importantly, indexing the driveshaft helps keep you from placing it 180 degrees from where it was originally.

Split the rear universal joint, leaving the rear yoke attached to the differential. Pull the driveshaft away from the rear of the transmission on cars that have a splined, tubular slip joint on the front of the driveshaft that allows it to change lengths as required when the axle bounces up and down. Other makes with the slip joint in the middle of the drive shaft will have an easy way to split the front u-joint, as well.

The next step depends on which u-joint your car has. The Spicer, Mechanics, or Detroit split-yoke

This is a rear, cross-and-yoke u-joint and u-bolts removed from a driveshaft.

This is the front slip joint that allows the driveshaft to change lengths as the car bounces over bumps. Once the rear u-joint is split, pull the driveshaft back, away from the transmission.

Retaining clips are removed first, then bearing caps are pressed out in a vise. Dress edges of yoke holes with a fine rat-tail file to remove burrs before pressing in the new u-joint.

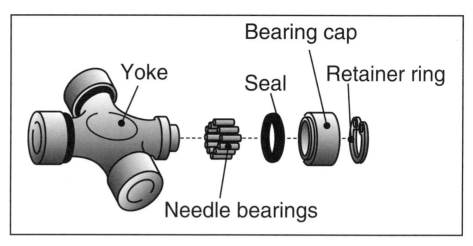

This is what a standard, pressed-in cross-and-yoke u-joint looks like.

Once the retaining clips are removed, the bearing caps can be pressed out using a vise and sockets. When that is done, dress the edges of the yokes using a rat-tail file to eliminate burrs.

joints can merely be unbolted and replaced. On these types of u-joints, simply bend the little sheet metal locking tabs away, then unbolt the u-bolts or bearing caps. Tape the old u-joint together as you remove it so you won't spill the tiny needle bearings. Otherwise, you will end up skating around on them in your shop for the next month. Put a little grease in each of the new u-joint bearing caps, bolting them back in place and tightening them evenly. Using new locking devices, bend the tabs to secure the bolts. Install the driveshaft so it is aligned according to your reference marks and you're done.

Your car uses the more modern, pressed-in bearing u-joint (most cars made in the last 40 years use this type). To extricate u-joints from the driveshaft after removing it from the car, remove the bearing cap lock-rings using a pair of snap-ring pliers. Press the bearing caps out of the yoke for one arm of the cross, using a socket slightly smaller than the bearing cap on one side and a larger socket to support the yoke and receive the bearing cap on the other.

Slowly tighten your vise until the bearing cap pops out. Now do the same to the caps on the other arm of the cross. If you don't have a vise, use a hammer and brass drift to carefully tap the bearing caps out of the yokes. Inspect the yokes for burrs or ridges that might cause problems when pressing in new bearing caps. It is a good idea to dress the edges of the holes in the yokes with a fine, rat-tail file. Smear a very light coat of grease inside each bearing-cap hole in the yokes.

If your new u-joints have Zerk fittings installed to allow them to be lubricated, remove the fittings temporarily so pressure will not build up during installation. If the new u-joints are not greased inside, smear a light coat of grease in each bearing cap but don't overdo it. If you put in too much grease, hydraulic

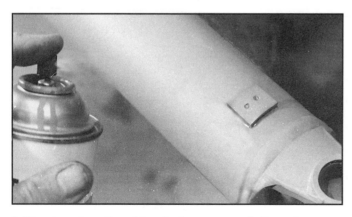

I like to give the driveshaft a coat of Rustoleum or Eastwood's Chassis Black to keep it from rusting. On many cars, to be completely correct, shoot the driveshaft with red oxide primer or Eastwood's Detail Grey aerosol paint to simulate bare metal.

Remove the Zerk fitting, if there is one, to relieve hydraulic pressure before installing the u-joint.

lock may occur when you try to press in the new bearing caps.

Install the new u-joint with its grease fitting hole (if it has a fitting) facing toward the driveshaft. Press in the bearing caps using your vise or a hammer and drift, being careful not to let the needle bearings slip around inside. Use sockets and a vise to press the bearing caps in far enough to allow you to install the retaining clips. Test your u-joints to make sure they are free and feel right before putting the driveshaft back in the car.

Take your car out for a test drive. If there is a minor imbalance in the driveshaft causing slight vibration, a large worm-drive hose clamp can be installed around the driveshaft and the screw mechanism repositioned until the vibration is minimized.

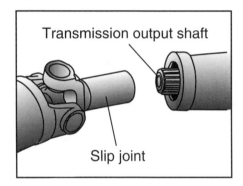

After splitting the rear u-joint, the front of the driveshaft usually slips back and off.

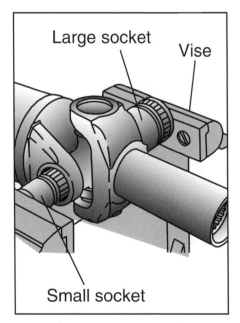

Press out the old joint using a small socket to press on one bearing cap and a large socket to receive the other cap.

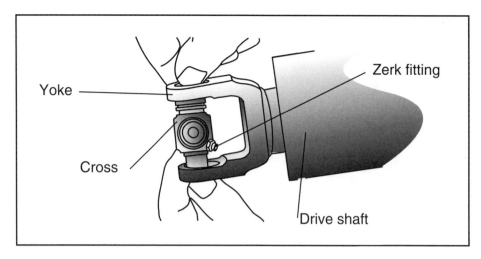

Install a Zerk fitting so it tilts toward the driveshaft front and rear. Not all u-joints have Zerk fittings.

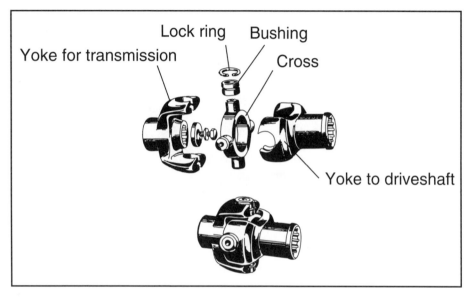

Fords, Buicks, and Chevrolets used a torque tube and single, enclosed u-joint for many years. This is a pre-1949 Ford joint.

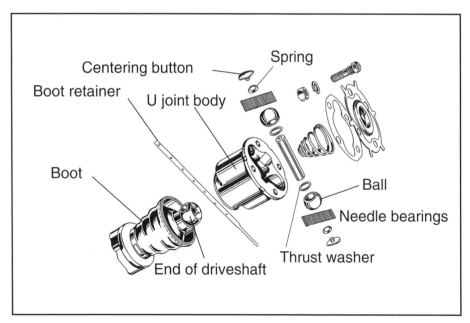

Mopar cars in the '40s and '50s used a ball and trunnion front u-joint. Rebuild kits are available through Mopar clubs.

Engine & Chassis DETAILING

Brakes

Going through the brake system is one of the most important parts of chassis restoration. Luckily, it's one of the easier tasks you'll face. The job doesn't require expensive tools and can be done by the home hobbyist in a couple of days. Hydraulic brake systems have changed little since the mid-1930s except for the addition of front disk brakes and dual-bore master cylinders for increased performance and safety. Here is how a typical old car brake system works.

Each wheel has a cast-iron drum against which two semicircular asbestos or other organic material-lined shoes press to bring the car to a stop. In the case of front disk brakes, drums are replaced by iron (or occasionally steel) disks, and the shoes are replaced by a set of calipers holding lined pads that grip the disk, stopping the car.

With drum brakes, the front shoes are called the primary shoes, and the rear-facing shoes are called the secondary shoes. When you step on the brakes, the master cylinder (usually mounted on the firewall or frame) actuates the wheel cylinders and engages the primary shoes first, then the secondaries — which actually do most of the braking.

Because of a car's forward momentum and suspension, the vehicle will nose-dive during stopping, especially with front-engined cars, transferring much of the car's weight forward. As a result, the brakes on the front wheels do more of the job of stopping the car than do the rear brakes. That's why front brakes generally wear out first and why front disks and drums have to be replaced more often than rear.

The brake shoes are attached to the brake backing plate by the anchor pin at the top and by spring-loaded brake nails at the sides. They are pulled in away from the drums by long springs when not in use. When the brakes are applied, the brake shoes are pushed out against the drums by hydraulic brake cylinders, usually at the top of the backing plate, though some cars have cylinders top and bottom. Adjustment of shoe travel is accomplished by turning the star-wheel adjusters at the bottoms of the backing plates between the shoes. See the illustration.

TAKING THEM APART

Put your chassis on sturdy jack stands. Pop off the front-wheel covers and the little dust caps over the axle nuts. Pull out the cotter keys securing the axle nuts and remove the nuts. Now pull on the front wheels to remove them — drums, bearings, and all. This method makes it easier to remove the front drums. Unbolt the drums from the front wheels.

Disconnect the flex hoses leading to the front wheel cylinders and drain any fluid into a container such as a coffee can. Disconnect the springs holding the brake shoe in place using the tool on the brake pliers. Now push in and disengage the spring-loaded, nail-type keepers in the middles of the shoes. Set the shoes out of the way and unbolt the wheel cylinders. If you intend to detail these parts, remove the backing plates from the axles.

Disconnect the emergency brake by rolling under the car and pulling out the pin holding the parking brake equalizer line running to the cables for the back wheels. This assembly is located about mid frame. The emergency brake cable system is the biggest difference between the front and back brakes on most old cars.

Remove the back wheels. Back brake drums usually need to be pulled off using a drum puller. There are two types in common use. The first, designed for most General Motors cars, grips the outside of the drum and pops it loose after a couple of sharp blows on the center of the puller. The second type of puller is used for most old Chrysler cars, as well as some other makes. It pulls the drum off by its studs and should never be struck in the center. Striking the center could damage the differential. Eastwood sells a third type which looks like a three-arm puller

with a difference. After tension is applied, the ends of the arms are lightly tapped with a hammer to release the drum.

Disassemble the back brakes the same way you did the front brakes. Use a brake tubing wrench to loosen the back brake tubing nipples. Don't try to do this with a standard, open-end wrench because you may round off the nuts. Tap on the nipples with a small hammer, shooting a little penetrating oil on them to loosen them. If the tubing wrench rounds them off, a vise grips may be your last alternative. When you remove the back-wheel cylinders, don't mix them with the front ones. Chances are they are different diameters, with the front wheel cylinders being slightly larger.

The master cylinder is the final component to be removed. On many cars made beginning in the mid-'50s, it is in the firewall and is easily extricated from the vehicle by disconnecting tubing and unbolting. Older vehicles often have the master cylinder attached to the frame. These master cylinders are actuated directly by the brake pedal. If you have such a

vehicle, roll under the chassis, disconnect its pedal linkage, and remove it from the car.

HYDRAULICS

You will want to put new piston and rubber kits in the master and wheel cylinders. If their bores are badly pitted or rusted, replace the cylinders or have them sleeved with brass or stainless steel. That will make them virtually impervious to further damage. If your cylinders are only a little rough, use a brake-cylinder hone to clean up the bores. Don't try to remove deep pitting with a hone because doing so will multiply the amount of pedal effort required to apply the brakes.

To use a brake cylinder hone, chuck it in a variable-speed hand

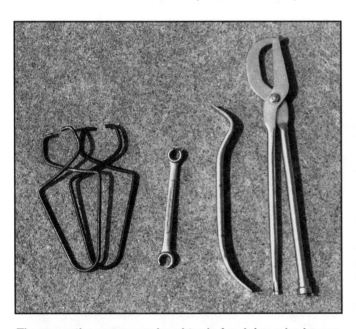

These are the necessary hand tools for doing a brake system rebuild. At left is a clamp for holding wheel cylinders together when shoes are removed. Next is a brake-tubing wrench, necessary for loosening hydraulic tubes. The S-shaped tool is a brake spoon for a shoe adjustment. The item on the right is a set of brake pliers for dealing with springs.

This wheel cylinder is so crusty we know it will be in bad shape.

Services such as White Post Restorations can sleeve your cylinders with brass or stainless steel, making them impervious to corrosion, especially if silicone D.O.T. 5 brake fluid is used in the system.

As we suspected, the cylinder is too badly pitted and grooved to be salvaged.

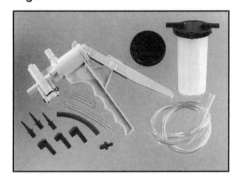

This MITYVAC tool from The Eastwood Company makes one-person brake bleeding possible.

drill, coat the cylinder bore and stones liberally with cutting oil, then slip in the stones. Spin the stones slowly in the cylinder, moving them up and down in the bores, but don't let them slip out at the ends. Keep working until all indications of corrosion or pitting are gone. Thoroughly clean the cylinder with alcohol-based brake cleaner before installing an overhaul kit.

Sleeving brake cylinders with brass or stainless steel, replacing brake tubing, then switching to D.O.T. 5 silicone fluid will pretty much end your hydraulic problems. There are several vendors who do this kind of work and who advertise in hobby publications. Here is one that has done a good job for me:

**White Post Restorations
One Old Car Drive,
White Post, VA 22663
phone (540) 837-1140**

Once the pits are removed, or once the cylinders are back after being sleeved, install new kits. Make sure your work area and your hands are surgically clean. One little bit of grit in a wheel cylinder can ruin it. Place kit components in a small container of brake fluid, then withdraw them as you need them. Use wheel-cylin-

Here is what the brake assembly looks like, put back together and clean. Now we just need to install the drums, then bleed and adjust them.

Be sure to top up the master cylinder before bleeding the brakes. Keep an eye on the level of fluid while working, too.

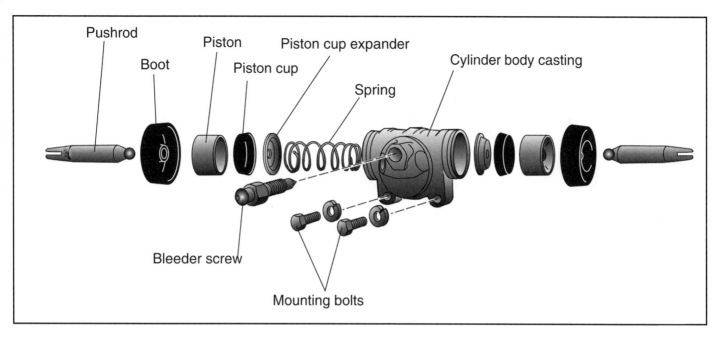

Here is a typical hub-type hydraulic brake system.

der clamps to hold the cylinders together until you can install them.

MECHANICALS

Brake drums that are lightly scored but do not cause a fingernail to hang up in the grooves can be cleaned by sanding with fine emery cloth. Drums that are deeply scored will need to be turned down. In that case, the brake shoes that go with them should be arched to match. Inspect your brake lining carefully. If it is black, glazed and shiny, or contaminated with grease, it will need to be replaced. If it is less than 1/8-in. thick it should be replaced, too, because it has very little useful life remaining. If your old asbestos linings are thick and healthy, leave them alone except to knock the glaze off of them with a little sandpaper.

The new, non-asbestos, organic-lining materials just don't have the stopping power of asbestos. N.O.S. (New Old Stock) asbestos-lined shoes can be found for some popular makes at brake-supply houses. If you can find them you are in luck. Otherwise, be content with the new types of linings. If you do obtain asbestos-lined shoes, or want to clean up your old ones, be very careful about disposing of any dust and wear a particle mask while working.

PUTTING IT ALL TOGETHER

Cleanliness is important to a good brake job. As noted earlier, hydraulic cylinders can be ruined by grit. In addition, oil or grease on a brake lining will ruin it. Try not to touch the lining with your hands, and keep drum surfaces clean, too. Use alcohol brake cleaner to rid either of even the slightest contamination, cleaning out any hydraulic cylinder couplings, tees, or tubes.

Clean, free up, and lightly oil the star-wheel adjuster mechanisms before installing them. Put a dab of white grease where each brake shoe moves on the backing plate. Replace any springs with new ones of the same tension. (As a rule of thumb, springs that are different colors have different tensions. Make sure you obtain the correct ones for your car.)

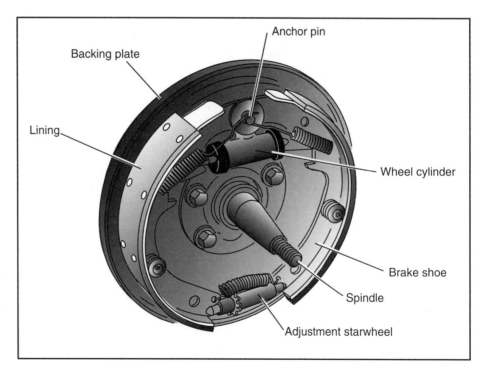

These are the parts of a wheel cylinder. Always keep everything spotlessly clean when working on hydraulic cylinders.

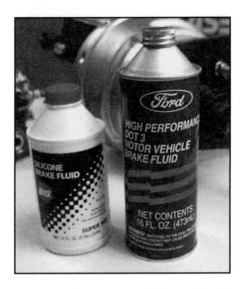

Silicone D.O.T. 5 brake fluid was developed for the postal system. Ford D.O.T. 3 conventional fluid is the best of its type because of its high boiling point.

Upper dual-bore master cylinder is for drum brakes and has equal chambers. Lower cylinder is for drum-disk brake combinations, has unequal size cylinders, and requires a proportioning valve.

BLEEDING THE CYLINDERS

Fill the system with brake fluid to the specified level in the master cylinder, then attach two feet of clear plastic tubing to the bleeder valve on the passenger-side, rear-wheel cylinder. Always bleed the cylinder furthest from the master cylinder first. Place the other end of the hose in a small glass jar with a couple of inches of brake fluid in it.

Have a friend pump the brakes slowly several times, then have him hold down the pedal while you crack open the bleeder valve just enough to let the fluid come through. Tighten the valve and have your friend pump the brakes again. Crack open the valve once more to release fluid. Keep the process going until you see no more air bubbles. Now top up the master cylinder, then do the same to the driver's side rear brake. Keep working in this manner until you have done all four wheels. Watch for system leaks while you work.

If you have no assistant, you can easily bleed your brakes with a MITYVAC brake-bleeding kit by topping up the master cylinder and then attaching the tool to the bleeder nipple. The tool can create 25 inches of vacuum and move about 1 cubic inch of fluid per stroke.

ADJUSTING BRAKES

Check a shop manual for your car to determine exactly how they are to be adjusted. The following instructions will work on all but a few cars, however there are some minor differences. Also, if your car has self-adjusting brakes, there may be some extra steps.

MASTER CYLINDER

Set the cylinder-actuating rod so there is about 1-1/4 inch of free movement in it before it starts to actuate the piston in the master cylinder. On many cars, there is a threaded portion on the end of the rod that has an adjusting and a locking nut to allow you to do this. Loosen the lock nut, adjusting it in or out to find the correct tolerance. Be sure to tighten the lock nut when you've finished setting the movement.

SHOE ADJUSTMENT

Jack the car up at all four corners and put it on jack stands. Using a brake adjusting spoon, stick it through the slot in the backing plate and rotate the star-wheel

adjusters down to expand the brake shoes out against the drums, or up to contract them. Adjust each of the car's wheels until you can't easily turn it, then back off until the wheel will turn with some drag on it. Install rubber plugs in the backing plates to prevent moisture. Take the car out for a test drive and readjust if the car pulls or if the pedal is too low.

ADJUSTING EMERGENCY BRAKES

Pull the brake cable toward the equalizer link. Remove any slack and adjust the clevis pins (the u-shaped pins at the ends of the cables) so that the pin will just enter both clevises at the equalizer link when the equalizer link is parallel to the driveshaft. Always install clevis pins with the heads up. Back off two turns on the clevis pins, then tighten the clevis lock nuts and install new cotter keys.

MASTERFUL MODIFICATIONS

If you are restoring a car to original for show, you will want to rebuild or replace the braking system exactly as it was when it came from the factory. Most old-car brake systems are surprisingly good when they are in top shape. Trouble is, most people neglect their car's brakes until they fail altogether, before doing anything to them.

THE SILICONE SOLUTION

One modification I would make to even a show-quality original restoration is to switch the system over to D.O.T. 5 silicone brake fluid. Silicone brake fluid was invented for U.S. Postal Service vehicles. It does not attract moisture like standard D.O.T. 3 fluid, so it does not deteriorate. As a result, the hydraulic-actuating system is much less prone to rust from within. Also, because there will be no moisture in the lines with D.O.T. 5 silicone fluid, it does not boil under pressure, causing brake failure by vaporizing from hard braking.

Front disk brake conversion kits are available for many popular classics, and are commonly used on street rods today because of their superior stopping power.

Ventilated drums can provide the stopping power of disk brakes for a fraction of the cost and weight.

The only problems with D.O.T. 5 fluid are the fact that it is about twice as expensive as standard fluid and, for it to be effective, the system must be purged and cleaned of old fluid using an alcohol cleaner before adding silicone fluid. Purging is not a problem if you are rebuilding the entire system anyway.

GOING DUAL BORE

If you drive your pre-1965 classic on a daily basis, a very good safety modification to your braking system is to install a dual-bore master cylinder. Anyone who has experienced total brake failure in an old car knows what I'm talking about. The emergency brake can save you if you get to it in time and if it doesn't throw you sideways by locking up the rear wheels. Often as not, you stop by colliding with something before you can reach the hand brake.

A dual-bore master cylinder solves this problem by having each cylinder actuate two of the car's wheels. If one bore fails, you still have two wheels to stop with. Most cars have one bore for the front wheels and one for the rear, but a few actuate brakes on one front and one rear wheel on opposite sides of the car. Either way there are big gains in safety.

Most older cars can be fitted with dual-bore master cylinders from later cars quite easily. Shopping around in hobby publications such as Hemming's Motor News and a

consultation with members of the club for your make of car should lead to the parts you need.

DROPPING IN DISK BRAKES

For street rods and daily drivers, disk brakes up front can add a lot to your car's stopping power. Complete kits for installation are available for about $1,500 from several sources for many popular

makes, and they are not terribly difficult to install. Disk brake kits may preclude using your stock wheels, however. On many old cars, disks can be a good addition, though they are not the only way to achieve better braking.

GOING VENTILATED

About 40 years ago — before disk brakes hit the American scene

Tools required to replace brake hydraulic lines are: Pipe cutter, tubing bender, flaring tool. You also will want to buy a 30-foot roll of steel tubing and the required nipples for your make.

Cut the tube to length using a pipe cutter. Tighten the tool, turning one full turn, tightening again and turning again until the tube is cut.

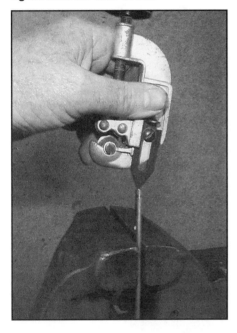

Clean the end of the tube using the deburring tool on the tubing cutter.

— a fellow named Mel Hamer in Southern California came up with the idea of vented drum brakes. He enjoyed running his street rod through the traps at El Mirage dry lake in the desert, but did not enjoy the brake fade and lack of stopping power his drum brakes exhibited at the end of his flying mile.

Hamer came up with a method of drilling precisely placed small holes in the drums to dispel heat and to sweep away moisture and dust. The technique worked startlingly well, eliminating drum brake fade. Hamer soon had a full-time business ventilating drums. But, you may ask, why would anyone want vented drum brakes when they could have disks and rotors instead?

There are several reasons. A lot less work and a lot less cobbling things together with vented drums is involved than installing disk brakes, for one thing. And vented drum brakes stop about as well as disks — sometimes better — for about one-third the price. Also, you can install disk brakes for around $1,500, or you can rebuild, ventilate, and update your car's original system — including a dual-bore, power master cylinder — for about one-third of that amount. You also will end up with about one-third the unsprung weight of disk brakes, and that's important.

The more unsprung weight a car has in relation to sprung weight, the worse it will handle and ride. Sprung weight is anything supported by the car's springs, while unsprung weight is anything on a car that is below the springs, such as axles, wheels, the steering mechanism, and of course, the brakes. Lots of unsprung weight is why trucks ride like trucks. A drum weighs about one-third as much as a disk, and a brake cylinder weighs about one-third as much as a caliper, so your car obviously will handle much better with its original drum-brake system.

Another thing that makes ventilated drum brakes a good modification is that they do not affect the originality of your car in a major way. They also are closer to the original engineering specifications, which is always important. If you decide to go with ventilated drum brakes, one way to do it is to contact Mel Hamer's successor:

Vince Bunting
C.H. Topping and Co.
520 W. Esther Street
Long Beach, CA 90813
phone (562) 432-0901

Vince has the original tooling to ventilate your classic's drums properly so they will be balanced and effective; he charges $35-$45 a drum to do the job. He takes orders by mail and ships anywhere

File the end flat, then bevel the tubing for flaring.

Bend the tubing to the correct shape using your old tubing for a template and employing a tubing bender to avoid kinks. Pop on nipples and push them down, out of the way.

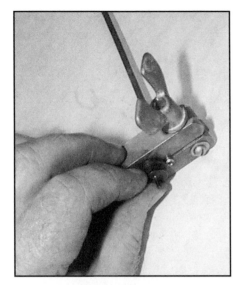

Measure the height of the flare using the bottom of the forming tool in the flaring-tool kit as a guide, then clamp the tubing in the holder.

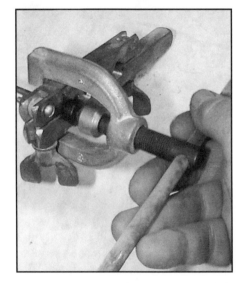

This is what the tube end looks like after the forming tool has created a rounded bell.

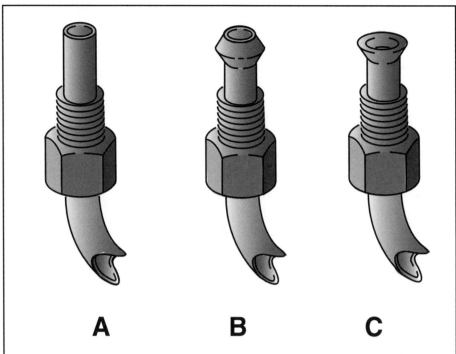

A   **B**   **C**

A) Tubing is cut square and filed flat.
B) Tubing is belled out using a special bit that comes with the flaring tool.
C) The tube is pushed in and double-flared using the flaring tool.

in the world. Call him for an estimate on your particular car's drums and for any brake parts you can't find locally.

DOWN THE TUBES

Most of us know that we need to go through the hydraulic cylinders and mechanical parts of our classic's brake system, but few of us understand how important it is to replace the system's hydraulic tubing. Rust and dents on the outside of tubing can weaken it and make it unsafe. Worse, conventional D.O.T. 3 brake fluid (D.O.T. stands for the federal Department

Of Transportation) found in most systems attracts moisture that rusts steel-brake tubing from the inside, decreasing its burst point even further.

Replacing the brake tubing should be part of any chassis restoration. It's easy to do and can go a long way toward making your restoration safer to drive. Replacement is necessary for cosmetic reasons, too, if you plan to show the car. All you need to do the job are a tubing cutter, a tubing bender, a flaring tool, the correct brake nipples, and the tubing. Tubing is sold in various lengths, but it generally should be purchased in 30-foot coils rather than trying to piece together individual tubes.

Hydraulic brake lines should always be made of steel. Copper tubing won't do because it does not have a high enough burst point. Brake tubing also must be double flared at the ends for extra strength. A single-flare tube can fatigue and leak. Bending steel tubing is easy if you have a tool to avoid kinking; for gradual bends you can even do it with your bare hands. Flaring requires a special tool available from automotive tool

stores or from The Eastwood Company.

Remove each tube from the chassis one at a time, then use the old tube as a template for bending the new one. That procedure will avoid confusion. Cut the tubing about 1/2-in. too long to avoid problems when flaring. Save any clips for holding the tubing in place, as well as any brass tees or other fittings such as are usually found on the rear axle housing and at the front of the chassis where the brake tubing splits off.

Cut the tubing to length, then file its ends flat and bevel the edges. Bend the tubing slowly and gently, using a tubing bender so as not to kink it. When you have it the way you want it, try the tube in its location to make sure it fits properly before adding nipples. After any minor adjustment you are ready to flare the ends. Pop a nipple on the end of the tube and push it down out of the way.

Now place the tube in the flaring-tool holder and make sure it sticks up at the right height by using the forming tool as a guide. Compress the forming tool over the end of the tube, then remove the forming tool and use the compression tool to finish the double flare.

Engine & Chassis DETAILING
Overdrive Transmissions

Want to make a highway cruiser with plenty of bottom end acceleration out of your classic? Consider an overdrive transmission.

Most major auto manufacturers offered electric overdrive transmissions at one point or another. Ford, Chrysler, Packard, and Studebaker made it available. Even G.M. — a company that traditionally avoided overdrive — offered it on mid-fifties Chevy cars and trucks. And some more modern vehicles made beginning in the seventies came with overdrive built in as a fourth gear. Chances are there is an overdrive unit to fit your classic too.

Overdrive gears allow your engine to run at less than a 1:1 ratio to the back wheels, saving up to 30% on fuel and engine wear. In the old days the term overdrive referred to devices produced by Borg Warner from the 1930s into the mid-sixties that replaced the tail shaft of a conventional three-speed and had in addition a two-speed planetary gear set in it.

A Borg Warner electric overdrive could automatically split second and high gears into two speeds each, giving you a five speed transmission. They were added to standard transmissions that you shifted conventionally in the usual three gears, but the overdrive shifted automatically when the vehicle reached a certain speed in second if you momentarily let up on the gas. Although you had to manually shift again into high, the overdrive would shift again automatically when you let off the throttle, to put you into your overdrive cruising gear.

These old-style overdrive transmissions are free wheeling, and even allow you to shift without a clutch below about 25 miles and hour. As a result they let you coast down hills without engine compression to slow you down.

Borg Warner made a number of models to fit different cars, and updated the design from time to time. There was an R6, R7, R9, R10, and an R11 at different times.

I have an R10 out of a '57 Chev sitting in my shop that will someday grace my classic pickup. An overdrive transmission from either a Chev car or truck will drop right in to a Bowtie car with a standard transmission from the mid-fifties into the sixties.

And overdrive can make a classic from the '30s, '40s, '50s, and early '60smore enjoyable to drive on today's freeways because it can allow you to cruise at 60 or 70 with your engine ticking over comfortably at around 2,000 - 2,500 rpm. Such a system still affords you plenty of low end acceleration too.

Old pickups were designed to haul heavy loads up steep hills, so they were geared low to cope with these conditions. Classics from the '30s and '40s were geared low to minimize shifting. As a result, today's 55 mph plus highway speeds really stress the engines of such vehicles if they don't have an overdrive. This can result in rapid engine wear, overheating, and poor gas mileage if you push your classic too hard.

At this writing, the going rate for a good, original overdrive transmission is about $200 to $500 including accessories. Just bear in mind that you need more than just the transmission to make the change-over if you want the transmission to work as it did originally. Make a list of the items you'll need, then check swap meets, and club and hobby publications to find the items. You'll be lucky if you find everything in one place.

GET THE COMPONENTS

When you find a likely candidate for transplant, take the side plate off and look at the gears and check the bearings, before purchasing. Also, if possible, actuate the sun gear governor switch on the side of the transmission using a car battery and a couple of wires. It should click audibly when it operates.

You'll need the kick-down switch that goes up on the carburetor and allows the overdrive to move back into a lower gear when you step on the gas, and you'll need the throttle linkage too, because it is not the same as on non-overdrive vehicles. And you'll need the lockout cable that mounts under the dash, and allows you to lock out the overdrive so you can use the transmission as a conventional three-speed.

One other critical piece to get is the relay that mounts on the fire wall. Without it the transmission won't work electrically. It is a good idea to take the cover off of any relay you find and inspect the points before you put your money down. If they are burned or pitted, chances are it is defective. They haven't made overdrive relays in years, so when you find a good one expect to pay between $60 and $175 for it depending on whether it is a good used one or N.O.S. (New old stock).

Finally, you will need the wiring subharness. These are easily obtained from sources such as YnZ's Yesterday's parts in Redlands, California (909) 798-1498. Be sure to tell the salesperson the year and model of your car and which transmission you have.

If you are lucky enough to find your overdrive tranny still in the car, measure and photograph where the relay, kick down switch, and lockout cable are supposed to mount. If you are not that lucky, you may be able to determine these things from another vehicle or an assembly manual.

INSTALLATION

These transmissions go in the same way as a conventional three-speed. Put your car on sturdy jack stands and check it for stability before getting under it. Split the rear U-joint and tape its bearing cups in place so you won't lose its needle bearings. Pull the drive shaft back and out.

Take the top two bolts out of your vehicle's bell housing, then find a couple of longer ones (6" is a good length) of the same diameter and thread type and cut off their heads. Screw these studs in to replace the top transmission bolts so they can act as guides when you pull your old transmission back and out. Disconnect the linkage and remove your old tranny. Shift your new overdrive transmission into third gear, then slide it into place. Turn the driveshaft a little from the rear to get the transmission to mesh with the clutch disk. Your old linkage and driveshaft will bolt right up on a vehicle of the same year.

You will also want to put your original transmission's speedometer gear in your new transmission so your speedometer will read correctly too. Usually cars that came with overdrive had slightly lower differentials in them, so if you stick with the speedometer gear that is in the tranny, your speedometer will read slow. Try telling that one to a state trooper.

Attach the kick-down switch to the carburetor and hook up the throttle linkage. Mount the relay in the correct spot on the fire wall, and the lockout cable under the dash in the correct spot. Adjust the lockout cable so it operates through the whole range of the lever on the side

The standard Chev transmission from the mid-fifties into the sixties is at the bottom, and the overdrive transmissions available in the tri-fives is on top.

Another overdrive option is to install a Mopar New Process transmission used with Mopar vans and some muscle car applications.

If you find an original overdrive, check the governor switch using a car battery. You should hear an audible click when it is actuated.

The solenoid is another electrical item that you should check before buying. Such items aren't being made any more and are hard to find.

of the transmission. Hook up the wiring according to the numbered chart and wiring diagram that came with the harness.

TRYING IT OUT

Start the car, get it rolling a little, then gently pull the lockout cable towards you to put the transmission into overdrive. Then as you shift into second gear and accelerate to about 25 miles per hour, the dash light will come on, signaling that the transmission is ready to shift. To

shift it, you merely lift your foot off the accelerator momentarily. This will give you a higher second gear.

When you shift into high gear, the light will come on again, and when you lift off the throttle, the transmission will shift into overdrive. If you have a sudden need to accelerate, stab the throttle to the floor, and the kick-down switch will take the vehicle out of overdrive.

If you decide you don't want to use the overdrive in hills because of its free wheeling feature, slow the car down to about 5 miles an

hour and push in the lockout knob. Once that's done, you can use the engine's compression to act as a brake as you would normally, but you will only have three speeds.

ALTERNATIVES

A company called Unitrax sells British Leycock De Normanville overdrives that can be adapted to many different manual and automatic transmissions. A typical installation costs about $2000 and mounts on the end of your car's

With any used transmission, you should check the slider gears for damage.

Check the cluster gear assembly in the bottom of the box for chipping and damaged teeth, because these can be hard to find too.

stock transmission. It is fully automatic and shifts itself. You will need to shorten your driveshaft to accommodate one of these, but there are services that can do that for you. If you want to go this way, call:

Unitrax
1280 North Sunshine Way
Anaheim, CA
92806-1799
(800) 630-4327

These overdrives are rugged enough for motor homes and off-road racers, so they are more than adequate for our classics. They will mate up to many GM standard and automatic transmissions, including the later Powerglide with the 11" tail shaft, making it a much more versatile transmission. They also fit many Ford, Muncie, TorqueFlite, and New Process transmissions.

Of course, if you don't want to go to the expense and fuss of installing an old style overdrive, you can look for a later four-speed tranny that will bolt into your earlier classic. I found that certain seventies-era Mopar New Process four speeds had an overdrive fourth and will virtually bolt right into most Chevys with standard transmissions.

This rugged, aluminum case transmission was designed for muscle car and van applications so you don't need to worry about damaging it in normal use. With your stock, classic-era 4:11 or 3:90 rear end you'll have plenty of bottom end grunt, but still have an overdrive that will let you cruise the freeways at more than the law allows in most states without taxing your engine.

You do have to have the front bearing retainer turned down on a lathe to fit the bell housing of the Chev, and you need to find a fine-splined rear U-joint yoke if your original is a course-splined one. Other than that it is a conventional installation, but it gives you a final drive of .73:1 which cuts your engine revs by almost 30 percent.

You will want to install the speedometer gear from your old transmission so your speedometer will read correctly.

If you decide to go with a Mopar New Process you will need to turn the input shaft bearing cover down slightly on a lathe to make it fit your classic's bell housing.

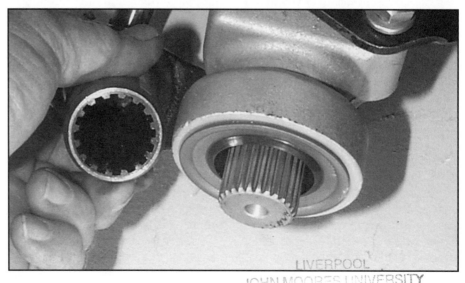

The New Process overdrive tranny requires a fine-splined U-joint yoke from a later Chev.

Engine & Chassis DETAILING
Differentials

Changing the gear ratio of your differential can make your classic more versatile, while rebuilding your rear end may be necessary to complete your restoration.

In this chapter we'll talk about rebuilding rear ends and about inexpensive and easily installed alternatives to your car's current differential gearing. The work will allow you to run with the fast crowd without compromising your classic's authenticity. On many older cars you can exchange the original differential for one from a different model or year of the same make that has a higher gear ratio, allowing you to go faster at the same engine RPM.

Or you can install lower gearing for more bottom end grunt. Here's how it works. Let's assume, for example, that the circumference of your car's wheels is 84 inches, which is what a 670X15 bias-ply passenger car tire from the 1950s typically measures. For each revolution of the car's wheels you move seven feet. Travel a mile and your wheels must go around approximately 754 times (5,280 feet divided by 7).

Let's further assume your transmission is in high gear, which is 1:1, or direct drive, and your differential has a ratio of 4.11:1 (in other words, the engine must turn over 4.11 times every seven feet), or approximately 3,100 times in a mile. So if the car is going 60 miles an hour (a mile a minute), we can see that the particular differential and tire configuration in our example has our engine spinning at 3,100 revolutions per minute.

Now let's look at what happens if we take out that low 4.11 differential, and install one with a 3.55:1 ratio. Again, our wheels must go around 754 times in a mile because our tires are the same circumference as before, but our engine spins at roughly 3 1/2 times that number instead of four, or 2,670 rpm if we are going 60 miles an hour, thanks to the higher rear end. The result is a 420 rpm savings.

To take the math a step further, assuming our engine's stroke is 4 inches (and it is a four-stroke engine), the piston must go up and down twice each revolution of the crankshaft, so

we can calculate piston travel in feet per minute this way:

Piston speed in feet per minute:

$$\frac{2 \times 4.00 \times 3100 \text{ rpm}}{12 \text{ (inches)}} =$$

2,066 feet per minute

The formula tells us that at 3,100 rpm, with a four-inch stroke, each piston must travel a total of 2,066 feet in its up-and-back motion. But if we cut the RPM to 2,670 by going to the taller gears in the final drive as outlined above, we can cut each piston's total travel to 1,780 feet, for a savings of 286 feet of travel per piston per minute. The result is much greater engine life and better fuel economy. Sounds good doesn't it?

So what is the downside to installing taller rear-end gears? Just this: All of your car's gears become higher when you install a higher gear ratio differential, meaning that if you have to drive up a lot of very steep hills and you have a big car with a small engine, your car may bog down and you will have to downshift much more fre-

HOW IT WORKS

When you go around a corner in your car, the rear wheel at the outside of the turn needs to travel further than the wheel on the inside. A small set of gears at the center of the differential called the differential gears (also known as spider gears) allows this to happen. When your car is going in a straight line, the whole differential gear carrier turns as a unit, and the little differential gears inside don't turn at all. When you go around a corner, these gears permit the rear wheels to turn at different rates. The little gears also allow your car to break loose in fierce acceleration so that only one wheel drives the car. If you are into red-light racing, a limited-slip differential is what you need to get both wheels going.

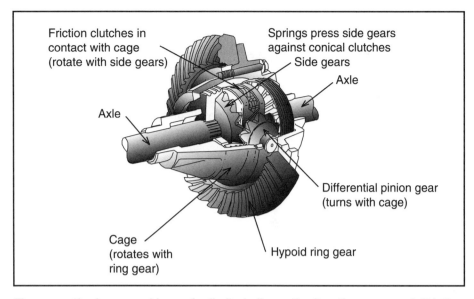

Friction clutches in contact with cage (rotate with side gears)

Springs press side gears against conical clutches

Side gears

Axle

Axle

Differential pinion gear (turns with cage)

Cage (rotates with ring gear)

Hypoid ring gear

These are the inner workings of a limited-slip, or Positraction, rear end. Friction clutches help distribute the power. A Positraction rear end was available on many muscle cars from the '60s and will help keep the back end under control under hard acceleration. Such a differential can be a good option for earlier cars that have hot engines.

quently. Nor will you have quite the off-the-line get up and go you had before.

But it has been my experience that a slightly taller rear end will make a '30s- or '40s-era car or a '40s- through '60s-era pickup much more enjoyable to drive on today's fast freeways. Okay, so you can't quite leave 'em at the light the way you used to. But you can run all day at 70 miles an hour with the engine loafing along at a comfortable RPM.

Here's an example of what I mean: I am currently restoring a 1/2-ton 1958 Chevrolet Apache stepside pickup with the standard, 235 cubic-inch, six-cylinder engine. This old hauler was probably a fleet or utility truck for a city parks department or a local oil refinery. It has no expensive goodies such

as a radio or passenger-side sun visor, and has only a basic, standard transmission. It also came with that 4.11:1 rear end that I used in the above example.

Such a low rear end allowed the old beast of burden to haul loads of sand up long hills using Chev's economical little six, but it also meant that the engine screamed in protest above 50 miles an hour. Luckily for me — a person who wants to use the old truck as a parts chaser and not for heavy hauling — in 1958 this same truck could also have been had with a 283-cu. in. V-8 and Hydro-Matic transmission, in which case the differential installed originally would have been a 3.70:1. So all I have to do to better my top end

and mileage is to find one of these rear ends and install it.

This is typical of a lot of makes of cars and trucks. If a car came with a smaller engine, it had a lower differential gear ratio in it than the same make and year with a larger engine. Also if a car was made in the '30s or '40s, it came with a lower differential than was used in later years. Often as not, the later "pumpkin," or differential assembly, will bolt into the earlier car. As a general rule, cars with automatic transmissions have taller gearing than those of the same make with standard transmissions.

Here are a couple of examples. Some early '40s Chrysler six-cylinder cars came with differentials ranging from 4.03:1 in the seven-passenger

These are Ford 9-inch rear ends, which come in ratios for every need. Somewhere out there is the optimum differential for your classic. Check junk yards and parts suppliers. Make sure gears are in good shape and bearings are tight and smooth.

To get the pumpkin (gear case) out, pull the axles a short distance.

Chevrolets have circlips inside the differential housing to hold in the axles.

sedan to 3.54:1 in cars equipped with the Vacuumatic transmission. There also was a 3.91:1 gear set available. If you coupled the 3.54:1 differential to Chrysler's 241 cubic-inch six and standard transmission you could cruise comfortably on the interstate all day long. But the 4.03:1 gear set in the same car would keep you in the slow lane, your engine working itself to an early death.

Corvettes made in 1958 could be had with anything from a 4.56:1, a 4.11:1, a 3.70:1, or even a 3.55:1 rear end, depending on how the car was equipped. That 4.56 rear end would have given you blistering acceleration from a standing start but would have cut top speed and gas mileage, assuming it was coupled with a standard three-speed transmission. The tall 3.55:1 was offered with the two-speed Powerglide automatic transmission in order to give it decent top speed. That would have cut into the Corvette's tire-shredding, off-the-line thunder at the

bottom end. Somewhere in those combinations is one that would fit your individual needs.

If you are building a street rod and are installing a four-speed or five-speed transmission with overdrive, you may want lower gearing in your classic's rear end. That way you can lower elapsed times at the local strip. The sooner your radical, high-revving engine can reach optimum torque, the faster your times will be. By contrast, tall rear end gears could make the engine bog down before it reached optimum RPM. If you want to go to the expense of installing a Ford nine-inch rear end, you can have nearly any ratio you want, or ratios for different occasions. That's because there are so many combinations made for this rear end, and they are so easy to work on.

You can determine which ratio best suits your needs no matter what car you have by checking the specifications page in your shop manual. Finding another differential for your car with a more favorable gear ratio might take a little looking, but they're usually out there unless you are restoring a '53 Kaiser Manhattan, for example. Try junk yards, swap meets, and club publications, as well as parts distributors that advertise in hobby publications.

When you purchase your differential, you'll want to get the correct speedometer gear that goes in the back of the transmission. Otherwise, the speedometer won't read right. Usually, if you find the differential at a junk yard or parts supplier, they can supply you with the correct speedo gear.

GETTING THE OLD ONE OUT

Again, get out the shop manual for your car and familiarize yourself with how the rear axle is configured. Some cars have the axles held in place by plates at the outer ends, while others, such as late '50s Chevrolets, have the axles secured by clips in the differential case. Some cars have a cover on the back of the axle housing that allows access from the rear. You will need to know how the gearing can be determined if you are going to have to take a differential out of another car. If you can take the cover off the back of the banjo housing, count the gear teeth on the ring and pinion gears to determine the ratio.

Begin the task of removing the old differential by placing a two-by-four between the brake pedal and the floorboard to prevent someone from inadvertently depressing the pedal

Before opening the rear end, clean the axle housing thoroughly to keep grit out of exposed gears and bearings.

If you need to replace the ring-and-pinion gears, mark the gear case bearing pedestals so you can get them back where they belong, facing the right direction, during reassembly.

Mark the bearing caps in relation to the bearings so you can set the orientation of the ring to the pinion gear.

Pry the keepers out of the way, or remove the cotter pins, then slightly loosen the bearing caps.

Unscrew the bearing caps, being careful to count the number of turns required. That way you can tighten them to where they were during reassembly.

INSTALLING A NEW RING AND PINION GEAR IN YOUR OLD DIFFERENTIAL

Sometimes you can find a new ring and pinion set at an auto parts store or parts supplier in the correct ratio, but then you have to install it in the differential case. This is a fussy job, better left to a pro if you are not a patient and careful person. On the other hand, the job is no more touchy than rebuilding an engine and is easier than rebuilding a standard transmission. A couple of weekends and a few special tools are required.

Follow the instructions above to extricate the differential gear case, then bolt your differential to an engine stand or mount it in a large, smooth-jawed vise. Grab a sharp punch and a hammer and mark the bearing caps and bearing pedestals in relationship to one another so they won't be mixed up when you reassemble the differential. Mark the big, disk-shaped, bearing-adjusting nuts in relationship to the bearing pedestals.

Loosen the bolts holding the bearing caps in place enough to remove the bearing adjusting nuts. Carefully count the number of turns required to remove each bearing nut, write it on a tag or piece of tape, and attach it to the nut. This will help get the bearings back into approximate adjustment when putting things back together. Lift the differential case and ring gear out of the differential carrier.

To get the pinion gear and bearings out, remove the u-joint yoke, then the pinion nut. Save any shims. Slide the pinion shaft out the rear of the differential carrier. Pull the pinion seal out of the front of the casting. The bearing and adjusting cone (if there is one) should come out next. If, after inspecting the bearings, you decide they must be replaced, drive the bearing races out of the carrier casting with a hammer and brass drift.

REASSEMBLY

If the pinion shaft needs a new bearing it will most likely need to be pressed on with a hydraulic press. Auto-parts stores and machine shops can help with this task.

When you install the new ring gear, tighten the bolts evenly in three stages to 45 lbs./ft. (This is a rule of thumb for most old car differentials, but check the shop manual to be sure. Yours may differ.) If the bolts were wired into place originally, rewire them with fresh wire during reassembly.

Slip the pinion gear into place and install the front bearing as well as any shims. Set the gear case back into its bearing saddles and, using new keepers for the bolts, tighten the bearing caps loosely into place. Install the bearing adjusting nuts and turn them back into place the same number of turns as when you removed them.

ADJUSTMENT

This is the most critical part of the job. If you don't get the relationship between the ring and pinion gears right, they will self-destruct. Also, if the carrier bearings aren't preloaded properly, they won't last. Some differential designs use shims to adjust the pinion gear and shaft in relation to the ring gear, while others use a cone of soft metal inside the differential carrier. Be sure to read about how your car's type of differential is to be adjusted before undertaking the job.

The big, disk-shaped adjusting nuts beside the differential carrier bearings adjust the ring gear in relation to the pinion gear. They also set the preload on the differential bearings. Check the lash, or free play, between the ring gear and the pinion gear using a machinist's dial indicator mounted on a magnetic base. (Usually, it should be between .003 and .005 inches, but check your manual for the figure for your car.) Use a little methylene blue liquid on the gear teeth to check for proper contact. The chart shows what to look for and how to tell when you have it right.

To set the preload on the differential bearings, use a large bull caliper, which looks like an old iceman's tongs. With the bearing caps still slightly loose, check the distance between the bearing pedestals with the bull caliper. Tighten the adjusting nuts equally so as not to disturb the ring-gear adjustment until a feeler gauge of the correct thickness (.010 inch is common) will just slip in under one tip of the bull caliper.

It is well worth the effort to recheck everything before popping the pumpkin back into the axle housing. Again, if the gear lash and bearing preloads aren't right, the differential will be noisy and won't last.

That's about all there is to it. Now you can get on the interstate highway and tour in the fast lane.

WHERE TO FIND THEM

A good supplier of ring and pinion sets for Ford and Chev cars and trucks is:

**Patrick's Antique
Auto Parts
P.O. Box 10648
Casa Grande, AZ 85230
Phone (520) 836-1117**

Patrick's sells complete rear-end rebuild sets with ring-and-pinion combinations in the correct ranges for today's roads. He furnishes everything you need except the dial indicator and includes an instruction booklet with his kits.

This is what the pumpkin looks like disassembled. Mark the bearing pedestals (top center) and large adjuster nuts before removal with a hammer and punch so you can get them back in the correct positions.

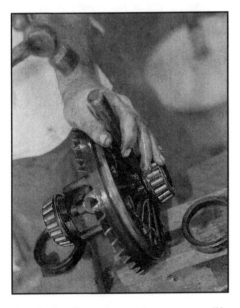

Bearing pullers are used to remove differential bearings, but a chisel can push the bearing out far enough to get the puller in from behind.

The pinion gear slips out the rear of the gear case. If you must replace the bearing, press a new one on with a bearing press.

This differential was ruined by faulty adjustment. Note the teeth marks on the spider gear case and the worn and burned pinion gear. Proper gear teeth contact and lash are critical to differential durability.

while the rear brakes are exposed. Block the front wheels, loosen the lug nut on the rear wheels, then jack up the rear of the car, placing jack stands under the rear axle.

Remove the rear wheels. Next, pull off the rear drums. To accomplish this you will probably need a drum puller. Which type of puller depends on the type of car you have. Older Chrysler, Ford, and Packard products need a puller that attaches to the studs on the drums, but General Motors cars require a puller that grips the edges of the drum.

If your car uses the kind of puller that grips the edges of the drums, pound the center of the drum puller with a rubber mallet to pop the drum loose. If your car requires a puller that attaches to the studs, pounding the drum puller could damage the thrust block in the differential spider gears.

Disconnect the steel brake lines from the wheel cylinders and remove the brake backing plates if it is necessary to do so on your make. Save any shims between the backing plates and the axle flanges and don't mix them up. Next, pull the axles out far enough in the housing to allow you to get the pumpkin (gear case) out. On some cars, you will need an axle puller to loosen the axles. Finally, split the rear u-joint and wire or tape its bearing cups together so as not to lose the needle bearings inside.

Put newspapers or a large cookie pan under the differential carrier, then scrape off dirt or caked-on grunge. Wash the carrier with solvent and a brush. Don't allow any grit to fall into the bearings or gears when you pull the pumpkin. Your old differential is worth something to somebody and will

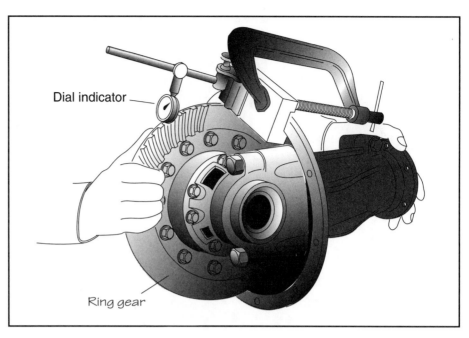

A dial indicator is used to check backlash between ring and pinion gears.

be good to keep as a spare. Drain the gear oil from the differential. On many cars, there will be a plug in the bottom of the axle housing to allow you to do this, but if there isn't, remove one of the lower bolts from the differential carrier to accomplish this task.

Roll the transmission jack under the differential carrier and run it up to just below the axle housing. Don't be tempted to lift the differential assembly out with your bare hands unless you are a weightlifter because rear ends are usually heavy and inevitably slippery. Cut the heads off of a couple of 3-inch bolts the same size as the ones that hold in the differential assembly to make a pair of studs. Take the bolts out at the 3 and 9 o'clock positions, installing the long studs in their place. Now remove the rest of the bolts and slide the differen-

tial carrier forward and onto your transmission jack. Strap the gear case to the transmission jack and roll it out from under the car.

Installing another gear case assembly is easy. Smear a little hypoid oil on the gears if you washed out the case on your replacement differential, making sure to pack the outer axle bearings and replace the seals at the brake hubs if required on your car. (GM vehicles lubricate the axle bearings with the differential lube, so there's no need to pack the rear bearings.)

Use a little silicone to seal the gaskets and tighten the pumpkin and rear access pan in place evenly according to torque specs in your manual. Fill the housing to the inspection hole with hypoid gear oil of the correct viscosity for your application using a ketchup squeeze bottle.

You can make a new gasket for the banjo housing by placing a piece of heavy fiber gasket paper over the opening in the rear axle, then gently tapping all around with a small ball-peen hammer to make an outline. Cut it out with a utility knife and hole punches.

3.70:1 differential in my old Chevrolet pickup will enable it to live life in the fast lane for a change.

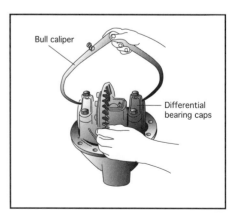

A large bull caliper and feeler gauge is used to check bearing preload on differential bearings.

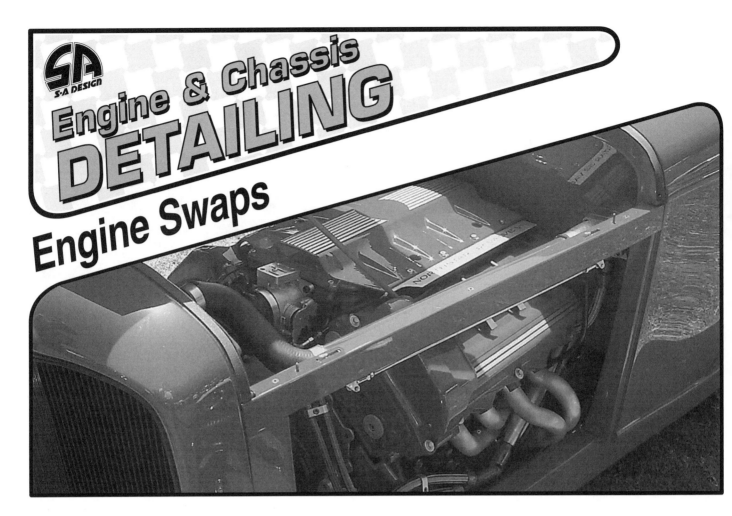

Engine & Chassis DETAILING

Engine Swaps

Are you planning to restore a car with a blown engine? I'm not talking about supercharging either. I'm talking about damaged. Dead. Gone. I'm talking about a motor with a hole through the side of the block, or an engine that has gone into melt-down due to lack of oil and/or coolant so everything is ruined, or an engine that is so rusted out that it can't be saved. If your engine is just worn and in need of an overhaul, chances are it can be rebuilt to be better than new, but if it is truly shot, that is another matter. Your classic is probably in need of a heart transplant in that case. Here are the alternatives:

THE EXPENSIVE APPROACH

If you are one of those meticulous restorers who wants to have all the numbers match, or you are driving a rare, early car, you may want to have your old block fixed and the engine rebuilt. In many cases a fracture can be welded, but the process is expensive. To weld up a cast-iron engine block requires a specialist, and the

block must be heated in an oven to cherry red first. This can cause warping, stresses, and other problems, so the block must then be remachined and align bored. If you decide to go this route, Excelsweld U.S.A. in Oakland, California (1-800-743 HEADS) can help you.

Of course, that broken rod may have damaged the cylinder bore too. Deep damage to cylinder walls can only be fixed by boring them away completely and wet sleeving the block. However, it is possible the reason an old engine self-destructed in the first place was due to overheating because of a corroded cooling system. Cylinder walls on the water jacket side rust away to the point where they are too thin to dissipate heat properly, causing the engine to fail. This happened a lot on old Ford flathead V-8s. Having a machinist install wet sleeves is the answer.

Cracked heads can be fixed too, but if the cracks are between valve seats, the repairs may not last due to the fragility of the castings in those areas. It is better to find a replacement head

in sound condition than to try to fix an old one. You'll most likely be money ahead, and you won't have to worry about problems later.

THE LESS EXPENSIVE WAY

Next on the list of remedies are new engines, crate motors, and long and short blocks. And yes, new engines can still be found for a surprising number of the more common classics. For example, if you need a small-block engine to fit in your '55 or later classic Chevy, you're in luck. At your local Chevy dealer you can get a brand new 350 with a four bolt main that will drop right in for $1,600 at this writing. It isn't exactly the same motor that was in a '55 (its internal displacement is a little bigger and it pumps out more ponies), but it looks the same, especially when you add classic manifolds and carb.

If you own a more common production car built in the last 30-40 years, call a dealership and see what is available. You might be surprised. In addition to engines that are still in production, there are N.O.S. (New Old Stock) motors stored here and there around the country too. There is nothing quite like a factory fresh mill. In the last few years I've seen a brand new '50s-era G.M.C. 270 still in the crate, a spanking new flathead Cad V-8 intended for a tank in World War II on its original skids, and a postwar Packard flathead six that was crated and still covered in protective coating.

The next level down are remanufactured or rebuilt motors. If you decide to settle for one of these, you can get the price down below a thousand dollars in many cases. Just remember that a rebuilt motor is one that has been repaired as needed. But a remanufactured motor has all new pistons, bearings, valves, and springs and has been machined to factory specs. Either choice can be fine depending on the company doing the work. It pays to ask around and to get a guarantee from the vendor.

THE SHORT AND LONG OF IT

You will hear the terms "short" and "long" block when checking around for rebuilt engines. A short block only includes the bottom end of an engine, or the block, crank, and pistons but does not include the heads, manifolds, or accessories. If all you did was damage the block in an otherwise decent engine, the short block may be just what you need, and in that case you can get the price down another $500.

A long block is a complete engine including heads and valvetrain, but you still need to use your old manifolds and accessories. The advantages to a long block are that you will wind up with a completely new engine, and it will save you assembly time. If you have more time than money and like working on engines, go for the short block. If you want to get back on the road quickly, go for the long.

SALVAGE YARD TREASURES

There is a surplus motor out there somewhere for just about any vehicle made in the last sixty years. In fact, there are actually more old engines than sound vehicles in which to install them. As an example, a few years ago, a 1914 American LaFrance fire engine was competing in the Great American Race when it blew a connecting rod near a small town in the midwest. They towed it into town, but figured that their race was over. As luck would have it, an identical fire engine was stored in a barn nearby. The crew bought it, switched engines, and after some frantic overnight wrenching, were on their way the next day.

If there are replacement engines for machines as rare as that, you can almost count on one being available for your classic. A few phone calls and shopping trips to junk yards, swap meets, and club get-togethers and you'll be back on the road in no time. Here are some examples I obtained just from calling around the Los Angeles area: How about a '72 Ford 351 Cleveland for $500? Or a '66 Plymouth 361 for $125? I also found a '55 Olds 324 for $150, and '57 Chev 235 six cylinder coupled to a 3 speed overdrive transmission for $200. The transmission is worth that much if it is in sound condition. Finally, I even came across a '39 Ford flathead, V-8 complete and running for just $500.

Whoever said one man's junk is another man's treasure knew what he was talking about. But just to make sure you don't buy a pig in a poke, take the time to carefully examine your perspective purchase. Here are a few tips on what to look for and what to avoid:

Don't accept a junk engine that has been hit in its vibration damper or timing gear housing. Such an engine could easily have a damaged crankshaft or camshaft. You don't want an engine and transmission combination that has been hit hard from the rear either, because the entire driveline could have been knocked out of alignment. Also, inspect the donor car if possible. If it appears to have been well maintained until an accident, the engine is probably pretty good. But if the car was sadly neglected or is worn out, the engine probably is too.

Most junk yards will start an engine for you if you ask, whether it is in a car or not. But hearing it run won't tell you much more than whether there are major problems. Look for blue smoke which is an indication of worn rings or leaking valve guides, causing oil con-

If this happens to you, try to find and save the piece if you want to repair the original block. If you don't, the welder will have to fabricate a new one at your expense.

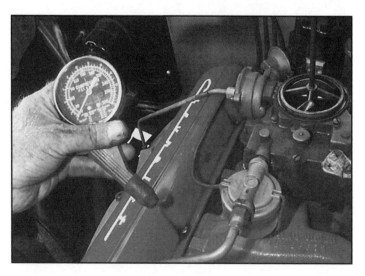

Check donor engines with a compression test if possible before writing that check.

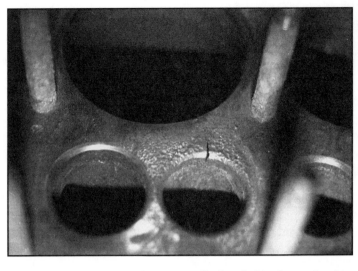

If the spark plugs in a junk motor look wet with oil and soot or are rusty from coolant, find another engine.

Cracks in valve seats or between cylinders in blocks are hard to fix. Look for replacements unless you are restoring a rare car.

sumption problems. Listen for rhythmic clunks, clanks, and bonks that would indicate rod or main bearing wear.

Then to really determine your prospective engine's condition, warm it up for 15-20 minutes, then shut it off, block its choke open, and run a compression check. To do that, you need to remove all of the spark plugs, and take out the coil high-tension lead so as not to start a fire. Of course, you will also need to know the correct compression spec for your car's engine, and that can be found in a shop manual.

Your donor engine's cylinders should be within 6 pounds of the specification. If the compression is ten pounds or more lower all across, the engine is in need of an overhaul. If the compression is down in two adjacent cylinders, it probably has a leaking head gasket or a cracked head or block. If the compression is down in just one cylinder, it could be rings, valves, a holed piston, or a bad head gasket. If, when you shoot a little oil down the cylinder and re-test it the

compression comes up, the problem is rings. If the compression stays down it is probably valves. If it only comes up a little, both the rings and the valves need work.

Look the plugs over too. If they are wet with oil or rusty, avoid that engine. Oil on the plugs indicates ring or valve guide problems, and water in the combustion chambers means a leaky head gasket or a cracked block or head. Finally, look inside the cooling system and around the freeze plugs for signs of corrosion. An engine that is extremely rusty inside will need cleaning out at the very least, and could have major problems.

Another thing to keep in mind while engine hunting is that you want the entire engine, brackets, manifolds, valve covers, carb, and all if it is coming from a car that is not the exact year and model of yours. Things can be very similar and yet not fit from engine to engine. It is a good idea to get the throttle linkage too, because bending new linkage to fit is no easy task.

HOT SWAPS

There is nothing more appealing at a show than a correct, original, restored car, but some such cars just don't make very good drivers. There are cases when the engine for your particular year wasn't as good as the one in next year's model, or perhaps your car is equipped with an anemic little six and you'd like to have the optional V-8 for that year. Well, you can, but it might be more complicated than you think.

Corrosion around cylinder walls robs cooling capacity. If the rust is bad, the block will have to be wet-sleeved to be used again.

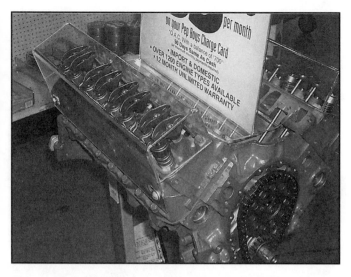

If you need a popular engine such as a Chev small block, some auto parts houses will sell you a remanufactured one for under $1,000 and even let you pay for it with monthly payments.

If you blew your Bug mill, relax. You can still get any of the parts you need to repair it, or you can purchase a brand new engine for a mere $600. PHOTO COURTESY SO. CAL. IMPORTS

That is because your original front springs, brakes, transmission, and drive line may not be up to handling the extra torque and weight of the bigger engine. Also, engine swaps are easier to do in some makes than others. For instance, the six cylinder early Mustangs are not set up to take the 289 V-8, and require replacement of a lot of components to do the job correctly. On the other hand, putting a small-block 350 in a classic-era Chev is easy.

Plan ahead, talk to people who have made the swap you intend to make, and be sure to get all of the accessories and linkage when you find your replacement engine. Just remember, the bigger and more powerful the new engine is, the more stress you will be placing on your classic's stock drive line. Another problem is that some unit-bodied cars have actually been known to crack from metal fatigue at their door frames from being twisted by a big

mill, making them very dangerous vehicles.

Good luck and good engine hunting. When installing your motor, work methodically, and double check that everything is hooked up right and that you have put fresh coolant and oil in it before starting it.

This looks like a '32 Ford with a Cadillac North Star engine, but it's an illusion. There is nothing Ford about it. Such a powerful engine would twist a real deuce like a pretzel. Putting a more powerful engine in your classic takes thought and planning.

This Morris is sadly neglected suggesting its engine has probably been similarly mistreated.

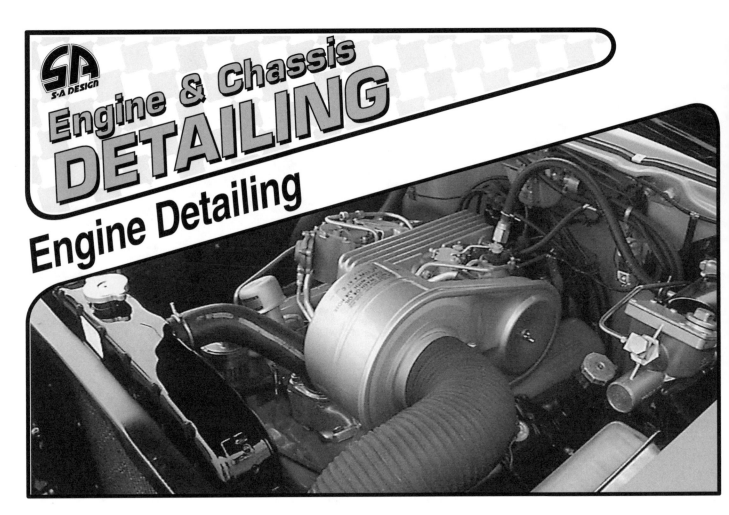

The time to detail your engine is after getting it back from the machine shop and before putting it together. You'd get overspray all over everything including the gaskets if you tried to paint the engine after it was assembled. Before beginning, order the correct colors and types of paint for your car's mill.

The items you sent out for machining, such as the block and heads, are already pretty clean because they were hot tanked at the machine shop. But the rest of the external engine accessories are probably as grungy as ever, so the first thing to do is to remove all of the paint, rust, and grease.

Caked-on grease and dirt can be scraped off using a putty knife and a squirt can of solvent. If the items are small enough, wash them in a parts-washing tub. Light oil and grease can easily be removed by scrubbing with a stiff-bristle scrub brush in a strong solution of laundry detergent and water.

STRIPPING PARTS

To get the last bit of grease and oil, as well as paint, off of the valve covers, pan, timing-gear cover, breather pipe, and other engine-room accessories, you can have them stripped at a commercial metal stripper, you can strip them with aircraft and automotive paint stripper, or you can immerse them in a bath of crystal drain cleaner and hot water. (Don't get the liquid type; it won't work.) This is essentially the same chemistry the commercial strippers use, and you can do it yourself at home.

Four cans of crystal drain cleaner in 10 gallons of hot water will rid parts of paint and grease quickly, and the stuff is inexpensive. The only problem is that crystal drain cleaner is poisonous and will burn your skin; the fumes from the solution can produce lesions on your lungs. Work in a place where neither kids nor pets can get anywhere near the stuff, and wear neoprene gloves, a respirator, and eye protection while you work. If you splash any of this witch's brew on you, flood the affected area with clean, clear water immediately to dilute it. If drain cleaner splashes in your eyes, or you or someone else somehow ingests any of it, follow the instructions on the can, then seek medical attention immediately.

If you decide to use a commercial paint stripper, the same rules apply. You'll need protective gloves and eye protection, you'll want to work in a secure place away from the kids, and in the case of paint stripper, wear a respirator to prevent lung damage.

Shoot on a heavy coat of stripper, then let it sit for 5 to 10 minutes. Scrape a little off using a putty knife or Bondo spreader. The paint should come off to bare metal. If it doesn't, don't keep scraping. Instead, shoot on more stripper and then wrap the part in sandwich wrap to limit evaporation. The paint eventually should come off easily.

BLASTING CASTINGS

In order for the paint to hold up on your bell housing, intake, and exhaust manifolds, you will need to media blast the rust and scale off them. If you don't have a blasting cabinet or rig, use an electric drill and wire wheels, but it will take a while longer.

A blasting cabinet and aluminum oxide are also good for stripping valve covers, pans, and other sheet metal parts, but you must be careful not to overdo it and warp and peen the metal. Also, make sure you get every last bit of grit out of the inside of a pan or timing cover because the stuff is death to engines.

TAKING OUT DENTS

Use a picking hammer to tap out any dents or dings in the valve covers, timing cover, or motor pan, then clean with a fine file. If you need to use filler to even up an external surface, get U.S. Chemical & Plastics' all-metal filler. Use it sparingly. Plastic filler will not hold up if it is thicker than 1/8-inch, especially under hot, oily conditions.

REMOVING RUST

Not even media blasting and brushing with a wire wheel will remove all rust, so it is important to give engine parts and accessories a liberal washing with Oxisolv or another rust remover and metal-etch solution before painting. Oxisolv also is good for removing heavy rust. See the rust-proofing chapter for instructions.

Finally, sand the bare metal with No. 80 grit sandpaper to develop a tooth for the paint to adhere to, then wash

the part with an etching solution such as DuPont's Quik Prep for maximum adhesion. Dry the part thoroughly with compressed air or towels before shooting paint. If you can't remove the rust completely, use Corroless Rust Stabilizer from Eastwood. This rust converter/excapsulator withstands temperatures of 500 F degrees.

PAINTING PARTS

Mask or tape cardboard over surfaces that should not be painted. If you are shooting engine accessories such as the generator, air filter, fan, or oil filter, shoot on a coat of metal-etch primer. Don't shoot primer on the engine-block castings. Primer causes problems with adhesion on engines because it can't handle the heat, so none should be used on the block, manifolds, pan, or valve covers. If you feel you must prime these surfaces, use Corroless Rust Stabilizer. It is a good idea to loosely install an old set of plugs when painting heads in order to prevent paint from running into the plug-hole threads. When shooting engine enamel, especially on unprimed metal, spray on a light mist or tack coat and let it get sticky before shooting on a full coat of paint. That way you will avoid runs. On the intake manifold, shoot on a coat of high-temperature silver exhaust paint. Let it dry, then shoot on the engine color.

High-temperature paint will keep the engine enamel from burning near

WHAT YOU WILL NEED

- Four cans, Drano crystal drain cleaner and a large metal wash tub
- Or: Eastwood aircraft and automotive paint stripper
- Neoprene gloves and harsh chemical gloves
- Eye protection
- Respirator mask with charcoal filters
- Blast cabinet (optional, but a real time saver)
- Engine enamel in correct color
- Semi-gloss black engine enamel
- Gloss black enamel
- High-temperature manifold paint
- Appropriate decals

where the intake manifold mates to the head and high temperatures are generated. Most engines were shot with paint during assembly, so you will probably want to paint engine fasteners such as pan bolts, valve cover screws, and their washers the same color as the engine.

Manifold castings should be given a coat of cast iron-colored, high-temperature paint. The bell housing was unpainted on many cars but should get a coat of cast-iron paint or be powder coated to keep it from rusting. Steel fuel lines should be left unpainted, as should the washers that hold down the motor mounts. Use a satin clear on such items if you like. Carburetor linkage should be cadmium plated on most cars. The bases of

This 1955 Thunderbird had a particularly beautiful stock engine room. Note the finned aluminum valve covers with turquoise emblem and the high chrome air filter. Also note that in 1955 Ford used a six volt, tar-top battery.

The 1964-1/2 Mustang 289 had a bright-blue engine and air filter. This car also has the rare air-conditioning and the correct caution label on the fan shroud. Shocks, which show up in their towers, are dark blue.

This 'Bird is correct down to its matte silver power-steering reservoir and bright-red windshield-washer bag.

The mid-'50s GM generator was semigloss black with cast-iron ends. (The Eastwood Company makes the correct color paint for this job.)

The correct period radiator cap is essential on high-point show cars. More important is that it be the correct pressure for the car's cooling system.

Always renew motor mounts when restoring your chassis. Even if they look good, chances are they have sagged and are getting stiff and brittle.

The bell housing on this mid-'50s Chev pickup was unpainted cast iron, as was the starter pedal linkage. The starter pedal was black. This one is powder coated for extra durability.

Hot Chevrolet six has old-style Wayne valve cover and side plate. These are polished aluminum and can be powder coated clear for extra gloss and durability.

A vintage flathead Mercury has all the trick equipment, such as Edelbrock aluminum heads and finned air filter. It also has a polished-aluminum intake manifold with twin Stromberg 97 carburetors. Eastwood makes a kit for polishing aluminum as well as stainless steel.

Late-'60s Dodge Magnum 383 cu. in. engine has correct, wrinkle-finish air filter. When shooting wrinkle paint, use no primer and shoot on three coats, the first going back and forth and allowed to get tacky, then another coat shot diagonally, and finally a third coat applied up and down. A low-temp oven or flood lamp helps the wrinkling process on cool days.

This rare '57 Chev fuelie has everything right, down to the semi-gloss silver air filter with appropriate decal, tar-top battery, wire hose clamps, unpainted master cylinder, windshield washer bottle, and shiny radiator.

many carbs were painted gloss black. Here again, powder coating would work well.

Let paint dry and harden for a few days before beginning engine assembly. Enameled items can be baked in a toaster-oven for extra durability, but keep the temperature around 160 degrees if you decide to cure your paint this way. The finishing decals for that final touch of authenticity usually are available from parts sources for your make and year of car, or you can get them from the club for your marquee.

That's about it. Now, when you put your engine back together, it will have a clean, neat, detailed appearance that will complement the rest of the restoration.

WHAT COLOR WAS IT?

This information is specific to the classic, tri-five Chevs but can help with other GM makes. (Information courtesy of Classic Chevy International)

SEMI-GLOSS BLACK:

Entire chassis
Rear-axle housing
Springs
Gas-tank straps
Shock absorbers
(mounting washers
should be cadmium plated)
Entire front suspension
Brake drums
Inner fender panels
Radiator
All panels behind grille
Starter
Generator
Water pump pulley and fan
Power steering pump
Ignition coil
Distributor body
Air cleaner (V-8)
Battery holder and hold down
(hold-down bolts should be
cadmium plated)
Entire underside of hood
Voltage regulator cover
Powerglide dipstick and tube

RED OXIDE PRIMER

Inside floor board
Inside doors
Entire underside of body
Cast differential third member
(some plants left these unpainted)

GLOSS BLACK

1956 and 1957 hubcap inserts
1957 rear bumper insert
Air cleaner (six-cylinder engines)
Headlight buckets
1955 and 1956 vertical quarter
moldings
Valve cover lettering V-8 ('55)
Tail light housing inserts ('56)
Horns
Bumper jack mechanism (post
is cadmium plated)
Bumper jack foot
Lug wrench
All bolt on pulleys

SILVER

Lettering on valve covers
('56, '57 V-8)
Wheels, '57 Bel Air

CADMIUM PLATING

All sheet metal bolts
Hood supports
Hood, trunk, door latches
Fuel linkage
Generator heat shield on
power steering
Coil bracket
Spring hose clamps
2-4 barrel and fuel injection
oil filler caps
Oil filler cap, 225 hp dual
four-barrel engine ('56)
Oil filler cap, dual four-barrel
engine ('57)
Oil filler cap, fuel injection
engine ('57)

UNPAINTED

Entire exhaust system, manifolds,
pipes, and hangers
Steering box
Master cylinder and cap
Drive shaft and u-joints
Transmission case, standard
and Powerglide
Front motor mount bolts and
washers
Emergency brake cables and
housing

SPRAY UNDERCOATED

Rear fender wells (lower half)
Front fenders
(underside, lower half)

BRUSH-ON UNDERCOATED

All body seams (underside and
covered areas)

BODY COLOR

Inside of trunk
Firewall
Wheels (Four wheels on car
should be body color on
outside, black semi gloss
inside. Spare should be body
color both sides.)

INDIA IVORY

Hubcap inserts
1955 Bel-Air rear fender,
chrome inserts
1955 paint divider strips
1955 front fender chrome
inserts (Nomad)

CHEVROLET ENGINE ORANGE

1955 and 1957 V-8
Crankshaft pulley
Generator top adjuster, V-8

CHEVROLET ENGINE RED

1956 V-8
Crankshaft pulley
Generator top adjuster, V-8

ENGINE GREEN

Six cylinder ('57)
Harmonic balancer

BLUE FLAME BLUE

Six-cylinder engine ('55, '56)
Harmonic balancer

BLUE

1955 V-8 oil filter case
1955, '56, '57 oil filter case

ORANGE

Oil filter lid ('55)
1955, '56, '57 six cylinder
oil filter lid

Engine & Chassis DETAILING
Custom Coatings

By far the largest array of custom coatings for automotive restoration is available from The Eastwood Company. Specializing in tools and materials for restoration work, The Eastwood Company has a big selection of original engine colors, chassis black, clear coatings, and hammertone and wrinkle finishes, all available in aerosol spray cans for the home hobbyist. Of course, most of these same coatings are now available in powder form to be used with Eastwood's Hot Coat system. Following are some examples of what is available.

TAKE A POWDER

By far the most durable custom coatings are those that go with Eastwood's Hot Coat system. For basic detailing there are satin, semi gloss, gloss and even mirror blacks, plus cast iron, cast aluminum, and wrinkle black finishes. Those are in addition to over thirty colors, plus clear and translucent shades that look super when applied over chrome or stainless parts such as valve covers and air cleaners.

HIGH TEMPERATURE COATINGS

Ordinary paint will not hold up for long on intake manifolds, and will burn off faster than you can apply it on exhaust manifolds due to the 1200 degree temperatures it has to withstand in these areas. But Eastwood has a line of High Temp paints that will hold up for years. There is a cast iron gray finish, called Factory Gray, that looks like new bare metal for that just off the show room look, and a bright silver if you want a brighter look. There is also a steel gray for a stainless appearance on your headers, and a satin black paint that mimics coatings used on some classics.

There is also an aerosol paint available for the rest of the exhaust system that will keep it looking new, making the difference at a show where your car will be competing with trailer queens. I carry a couple of cans in my detailing kit and touch up the exhaust system on the show field before the judges arrive.

BLACK METAL TRIM PAINT

Those of you with cars sporting blacked out trim are in luck because Eastwood carries primer and paint that is durable and provides that OEM appearance. This paint will adhere to stainless, aluminum, and even chrome if you want to go for a custom appearance.

REAL ZINC FOR GAS TANKS

Your classic's fuel tank gets more than its share of moisture and dirt thrown on it in service, so it is a real blessing that Eastwood sells an authentic looking coating containing zinc that will work over minor rust and will really protect your tank for years. Here again, it's a good idea to carry an extra can in your detail kit if you are going to show your car.

CAD PLATING

Finding someone who can do real cad plating these days is difficult. So many platers have gone out of busi-

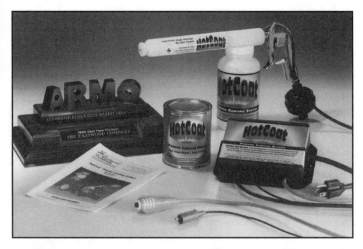

Eastwood's Hot Coat system applies the toughest, best looking finishes available, and is available in 40 plus colors.

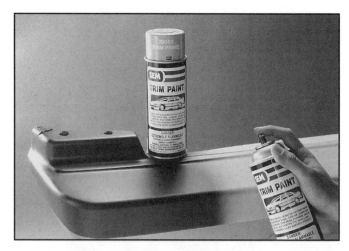

Is that plastic bumper looking tacky? There are special, flexible paints available to fix the problems.

ness because of strict pollution laws. Eastwood offers an aerosol coating that will give you a cad-plated look that is much better than just painting things silver, and will stand temperatures up to 250 degrees.

GOLD CAD

Do you want that old power steering unit to look the way it did when it left the factory? Well you can shoot on a little of Eastwood's Gold Cad system (it comes in four tints so you can get it just right) and it will look as good as new.

UNDER HOOD BLACK

This is an acrylic lacquer that closely matches that factory finish, and goes on thin enough not to hide casting details. You can buy it in quarts for big jobs, and then thin it with lacquer thinner.

CARB COATINGS

Gasoline will eat away most coatings, but Eastwood sells a bronze, as well as a silver aerosol paint that will hold up under the heat and the solvent properties of leaking fuel.

WHEEL PAINT

Are your rally wheels looking a little tatty? Eastwood sells tough wheel paint in aerosol cans in silver/argent, charcoal gray, and satin black. Over that, you can apply a clear coat to protect the whole wheel.

DETAIL SILVER

This aerosol paint replicates the subtle silver used on many car wheels, valve covers, air filters and other items. Ordinary silver paint looks garish; this paint looks right.

Most paints won't hold up on exhaust manifolds, but Eastwood's High-Temp will.

Looking for that OEM zinc-coated appearance? Eastwood's Tank Tone contains real zinc. Carry a can in your trunk for touch-up at shows.

Two ways to create that cad-plated look are powder coating with argent silver or shooting on Eastwood's Silver Cad.

That golden cadmium finish that came on your old power booster can be recreated with Eastwood's Golden Cad.

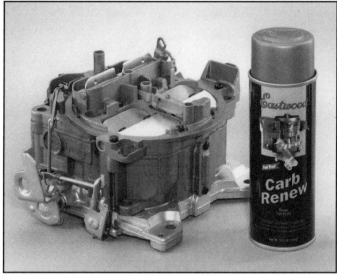

Under hood black is my favorite. It's the color and gloss most things were in the engine compartment.

Want that carb to look factory fresh? Use carb renew.

HAMMERTONE PAINTS

This style of finish is common on many foreign cars, as well as on tools, heaters, and other accessories. These paints have high quality resins, glass, and aluminum particles in a quick drying solvent that provides a tough, corrosion resistant coating.

WRINKLE FINISH PAINTS

Many radios, heaters, and other accessories in older cars had wrinkle finish paint on them. Eastwood sells the correct paint in black or brown. This paint is applied directly to clean, bare metal. Shoot on a coat moving horizontally across the item, then vertically, then diagonally, letting each coat get sticky before applying the next. Then put the part out in the sun or in front of a heat lamp to dry, for best results.

LETTERING PAINTS

Want to try pinstriping? Then you'll need a striping sword or Beugler striping tool and 1 Shot sign painter's enamels. This high quality enamel covers in one coat, flows out well, and holds up nicely.

BLACK OXIDE FINISH

Not a paint but a process that duplicates the original corrosion resistant coating used on many classics, this system is easy to use and holds up nicely.

PLATING SYSTEM

Looking for an inexpensive plating system for chassis detailing that you can use at home? Well, Eastwood makes one. This is not a paint but a tin/zinc plating system that resists corrosion and closely mimics chrome.

VINYL COATINGS

Have you repainted your classic so the upholstery no longer matches? Eastwood sells coatings that are durable and will allow you to change the color of your vinyl interior to match. It comes in 12 colors, plus gloss and low luster clear, and a primer.

Wheels looking tatty? Eastwood's special formula wheel paint holds up well and looks great.

Eastwood's detail silver has that subtle, clean look of original factory finishes.

Control rust and create an original look with these great hammer-tone coatings.

Wrinkle finish matches the original finish used in many classics. Shoot it on with no primer, then bake it under a heat lamp, or put it in the sun to help wrinkling.

One Shot sign painter's enamel is what pros use for pinstriping. It has a super high pigment content and covers in one coat.

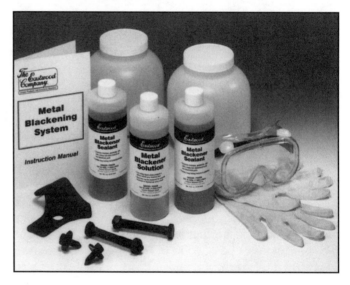

Eastwood even sells a kit to recreate that black anti-rust coating that came on many cars from the '60s and later.

Yes, you can change the color of your vinyl upholstery and it will hold up well. Use Eastwood's vinyl and plastic color spray.

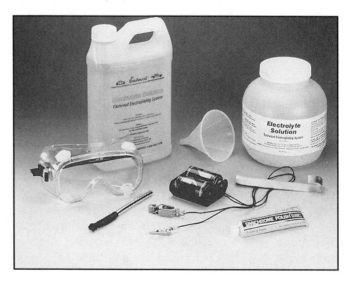

Get a brilliant, chrome-like appearance plus durability at home with Eastwood's tin-zinc plating kit.

Engine & Chassis DETAILING

Polishing

The great classic car makers such as Duesenburg, Marmon, Cadillac, and Packard used to detail and polish the engine components of their cars to the same perfection as they did their exterior paintwork, but that practice died with the advent of depression of the 1930s. These days, even expensive luxury cars look pretty businesslike under the hood. Too bad. Some of those early engines were as beautiful as fine Swiss watches.

The only people — other than restorers — who are doing that kind of dazzling detailing today are street rod builders. In fact, some of the engine rooms of street rods are true works of art. They are so dazzling that they can lure you down the show field just to have a look at them. Of course, to get an engine to that kind of perfection takes time and care, but luckily it is not difficult to master the skills, nor are the tools to do it expensive. If you want to set a shining example with your classic's engine, here's how it's done:

POLISHING VERSUS BUFFING

Let's start by getting our terms straight. Polishing is what you do to make a rough surface smooth. It involves removing material. Buffing is what you do to get that dazzling luster AFTER you've done the necessary polishing. In fact, polishing often begins with some fairly aggressive grinding and sanding. But buffing is how you develop the final "color" of the metal.

CAST-IRON BLOCKS AND HEADS

Many engine detailers take the time to grind and file the rough surfaces of engine blocks, heads and cast-iron manifolds to get them smooth for painting. Iron is hard, so doing this can be slow going, but beautiful results are possible. A series of cylindrical and tapered grinding stones or cutting tools are required, as is a hand-held grinder and a flexible shaft, or if you can afford it, a flexible shaft with a 1/3 horsepower motor. This set up will really make the job easy.

After you have cleaned away all the roughness and filed away slag and casting lines, give your disassembled engine a couple of coats of engine enamel in the correct color, or the color you think will compliment it best. Use cardboard and masking tape to keep paint out of areas that should not be painted. No primer is necessary with engine enamels, but to avoid runs, shoot on a foggy mist of paint, then let it get tacky before shooting on a good, wet coat. As soon as this flashes over (gets almost dry to the touch) shoot on a final coat of paint.

ALUMINUM MANIFOLDS AND VALVE COVERS

Ruff Stuff

Aluminum is soft, so it is easy to clean up and polish. File and clean away any slag or obvious roughness. Clean the surface to be buffed with a media blaster and glass beads, then go to 220 grit sandpaper on a rubber expander wheel to smooth ridges and

High speed buffer (3,600 rpm and 1/3-3/4 horsepower works very well)

Buffing wheels (sisal, sewn cotton, open cotton, and others as required.)

**Buffing compounds
(see table on page 109)**

Small, hand-held grinder/buffer and bits

Eastwood's PRE, Metal Wash, or lacquer thinner

Flexible cable drive

Files (Coarse and fine) **Face shield** **Particle masks**
Soft rags **Tight leather gloves**

The Eastwood Company sells complete polishing and buffing kits for any type of metal for $84.99 - $94.99 that have everything you need for engine part polishing including a step-by-step video on how to do it.

Most buffers are powerful enough to do serious injury, so be sure to follow these safety tips.

1) Dress properly. Fairly tight fitting leather gloves (available at welding supply stores) and a long-sleeved shirt are important to protect your hands and to prevent hot particles from burning your skin.

2) A full face shield and a dust respirator or at least a particle mask are also important to protect your eyes and lungs.

3) Hold the part under the wheel, never on top of it. A 1/2 horsepower motor spinning at 3,000 rpm can eject an item at very high velocity.

4) Brace long, slim items with a wood slat backing to stiffen them and keep them from slipping out of your hands. Never look away from your work while buffing.

5) Never put your fingers in holes to hold parts. Grinders and buffers have been known to rip items out of your fingers, and many stainless steel and sheet metal parts have sharp edges.

6) Never polish or buff a part with its edge in front of the wheel. Turn the part around so the edge follows the direction of the wheel's rotation. Buffers can grab an item unexpectedly and throw it at great speed.

7) If you have long hair, tie it back or wear a cap. Hair can get twisted around spinning shafts with disastrous results.

8) Press lightly. Let the buffer do the work. If you press too hard you just create more heat, and you run the risk of loosing control of the item to be buffed.

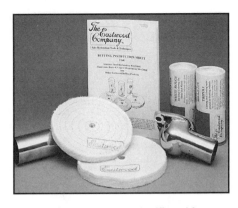

Aluminum and brass buffing kits are inexpensive and have everything you need to get the job done.

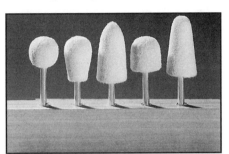

Felt cones are the best option for getting into crevices. Buy an assortment.

Abrasive tapers are great for smoothing out tight places.

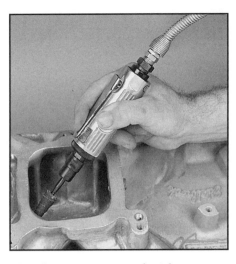

Abrasive tapers are perfect for removing roughness and casting slag from manifolds.

A Baldor high-speed buffer makes polishing even this blower housing a piece of cake.

mold lines further. Get into tight places using abrasive tapers and cylinders and a flexible shaft, either attached to your drill, a hand-held grinder, or ideally, attached to a 1/3 horsepower electric motor.

Polishing

Switch to a spiral-sewn wheel and 80 grit greaseless compound. Let the wheel sit for 10-15 minutes so the compound can harden before starting. To improve wheel flexibility, tap buffing wheel with a screwdriver handle before starting. Buff the part in one direction, clean the wheel with a buffing rake, then apply compound and buff at 90 degrees or as close as possible to right angles. Wash the part clean using lacquer thinner or Eastwood's PRE. If you

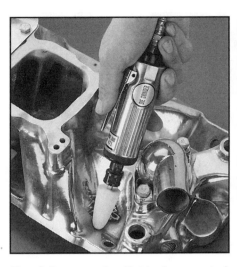

Use felt cones (available in assorted shapes) for final polishing on complex items such as aluminum manifolds.

Assorted polishing and buffing compounds are available from The Eastwood Company to make any type of metal shine.

are using a water soluable greaseless compound, it is best removed with detergent and hot water or Eastwood's Metal Wash. Now switch to 220 grit and repeat the process. Let the part cool frequently as you work.

To get into tight places, use buffing bobs and a flexible shaft. You need a separate wheel or bob for each type of compound so it will not be contaminated by the coarser compound. In the case of intake manifolds, a complete kit especially designed for the job is available from The Eastwood Company for $49.99 and will take all the guess work out of the job. I prefer to powder coat intake manifolds with Hot Coat clear, but if you want to use a conventional coating, you can get Eastwood's manifold kit — including a can of Nyalic Clear Coat Barrier — for $54.99

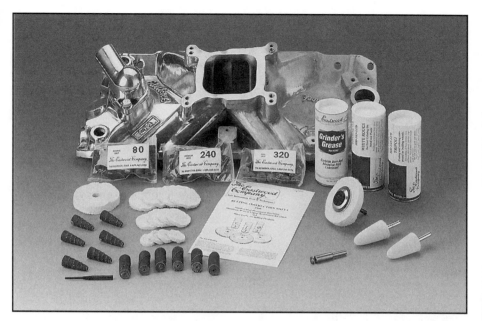

Eastwood's aluminum manifold polishing kit comes with grinding rolls, a mandrel and an arbor, plus all the compounds you need.

Nyalic Mag Wheel Protector provides a durable, clear coating for polished parts that won't be powder coated.

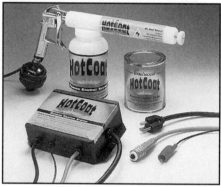

Eastwood's powder coating system provides the toughest custom coatings available.

Eastwood's PRE is excellent for removing dirt, wax, grease, and oil from body work before painting.

Metal wash converts slight flashover rust and etches metal in preparation for primer coats.

If your wheels are looking a little rough around the edges, relax. Restoring them is easier than you might think.

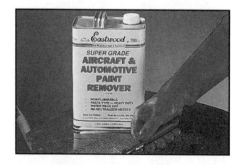

Use Eastwood's Aircraft and Automotive Paint Remover to quickly take off built up coats of old paint.

Proper lighting is essential to buffing and polishing. Use a single light bulb and tip the work at angles to show up every little scratch, or take the part outdoors and check it to monitor your progress. Don't polish or buff in any one spot for long, because heat builds up rapidly and scorches and discolors the metal.

For aluminum all you need to finish the job is a loose-section cloth wheel and white rouge. Clean the part with lacquer thinner or PRE before starting. Work a small area until done, then go on to the next. Again, change your angle of attack by about 90 degrees whenever changing grit or compound wheel combinations. Finish by lightly buffing in the direction of the longest length of the piece or along highlight lines for that dazzling look.

ALUMINUM WHEELS

The task of polishing wheels is much like manifolds and valve covers. First clean the wheel of dirt, wax and road tar. Detergent and water, or Eastwood's PRE are good for this job. Next, use paint stripper to remove any paint, powder coating, or clear coating. Wear heavy neoprene gloves and a paint mask while doing this because paint stripper can be hard on your skin and your lungs if inhaled. Finally, flush the wheel carefully with cold water to remove any vestige of stripper.

Remove any bead damage, nicks, or scratches using fine files and sandpaper. Blend out the blemish into the surrounding area to an 80-120 grit sandpaper finish. Now mount a 4" spiral buffing wheel on a flex shaft (2,500 rpm minimum) then apply 80

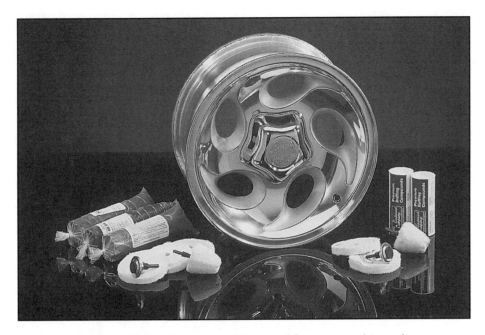

Eastwood's wheel refinishing kits provide everything you need to make your wheels look dazzling.

A flexible shaft coupled to a 1/3 horse motor are the ticket for polishing wheels.

Aluminum oxide is a long-lasting blast medium that works well to remove corrosion from harder metals.

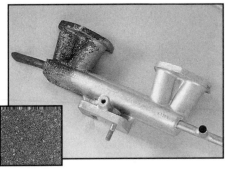

Glass beads are a somewhat less aggressive blast medium that is perfect for aluminum castings and softer metals.

Use Mag Wheel Protector to keep your wheels looking new for years to come.

grit compound and follow the instructions for buffing manifolds and valve covers. You may want to stop at a 320 grit satin finish rather than a high luster if you prefer that look.

A mirror finish can be done using a new, 4" loose section wheel and white rouge. Clean the wheel with

Eastwood's Scotch Cal Paint protects wheels and other vulnerable surfaces with a clear urethane that can be peeled off later without damaging the paint underneath.

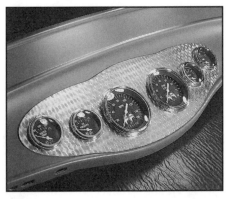

Engine-turned dashboards and fire-walls were popular on the great classics and still look gorgeous today.

PRE afterwards to remove any compound residue. Coat your wheels with Eastwood's Nyalic Mag Wheel Protector, or powder coat them with a clear Hot Coat for maximum protection. You can also powder coat using red, blue, or yellow for that anodized look.

A coarser satin finish can be achieved by blasting your wheels with glass beads or aluminum oxide. Mask off any areas you want to keep with a mirror finish using Scotch Cal resist tape. Aluminum oxide will give a coarser finish than glass beads. Test them both in an inconspicuous area such as the inside of the wheel to determine which effect you want.

ENGINE TURNING

This technique was often used on instrument panels and firewalls in the classic era to produce a beautiful jewel-like effect. (The process is also called damascene.) You will need a drill press or a very accurate eye to do this right, but it isn't difficult. Eastwood sells kits for $17.99 - 24.99 depending on what style you want.

STAINLESS STEEL

Removing Dents

Use a body hammer, or one of the special little hammers designed for working stainless available from The Eastwood Company to pick out any dings. Work from the outer edges of dents in toward the center, to help draw in the metal. Don't tap very hard, and use a small anvil or the tail of a vise to back your work so you won't stretch the metal and make new dents.

Use a fine file to carefully clean up any pimples. If you find small, low spots while filing, tap them out before going further. Only file enough to level the high spots. And be careful not to take off too much metal and weaken the part.

Polishing and Buffing

Next, take out the file scratches using a rubber expanding wheel and 220 grit sandpaper. Work at right angles to the scratches so as not to make them worse. When the file marks are all gone, switch to 320 grit paper, then finish with 400 grit. Be sure to sand in a criss-cross fashion, moving the part back and forth, to minimize the scratches.

Finally it is time to buff your part to a high gloss. Use a sisal wheel with emery compound and high speed buffer that turns at 3600 rpm to take out the sandpaper lines. Just briefly touch the wheel with a little heavy-

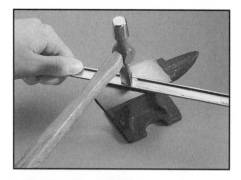

A small body hammer especially made for stainless trim is ideal for taking out dents.

duty compound made especially for buffing stainless, and then start moving the part lightly back and forth across the wheel, letting the spinning wheel — not pressure — do the work.

Let the part cool after each buffing, then clean it carefully with lacquer thinner so you won't contaminate the next polishing wheel, go to a softer, spiral-sewn cotton wheel and stainless compound and work at right angles to your previous polishing.

Let the part cool again, then clean it and do the final buffing using white rouge and an open loose wheel. Store your buffing wheels separately in sealed plastic bags with compound to avoid contaminating them with the wrong compound or dirt.

If you follow these simple tips and work carefully, even old, dented, and dull stainless can be made to look as good as when it came from the factory.

A rubber expanding wheel and a selection of sandpaper loops will make short work of smoothing jobs.

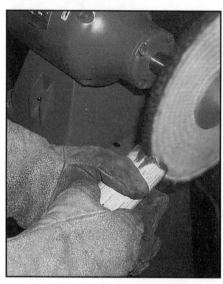

Only lightly apply compound to buffing wheels. Too much compound will cause dragging and black streaks.

BUFFING WHEEL AND COMPOUND SELECTION CHART

MATERIALS	Steel, iron, stainless, or other hard materials	Brass, copper, aluminum, die cast, zinc	Chrome, nickel plate	Solid and plated gold and silver	Plastics
Step 1 Rough Compound buff	Emery Sisal	Tripoli Spiral/ventilated	N/A	N/A	N/A
Step 2 Intermediate Compound buff	Stainless Spiral/ventilated	N/A	Stainless Spiral	N/A	N/A
Step 3 Final Compound buff	White rouge Loose section	White rouge Loose section	White rouge Loose section	Jeweler's rouge Flannel	Plastic Flannel String
Recommended RPM for 4"-10" wheels	3,600	3,600	3,600	1,800-3,600	1,800

Engine & Chassis DETAILING

Gas Tanks

Sooner or later, most collector car owners are faced with fuel tank problems. Whether you are doing a complete restoration, building a hot rod, or just refurbishing, you will want to clean and seal the gas tank before potentially disastrous problems strike. There is not a lot to doing it and it requires no special tools. But you do have to be extra careful because gasoline is as dangerous as dynamite.

Gas tanks deteriorate for several reasons. Oddly enough, the major problem isn't rust-out from water splashing onto the exposed underside. If tanks rust from the outside, it usually is due to water running down on them through the car's bodywork and chassis. But the main problem with old fuel tanks is internal. As fuel is pulled from the tank by the fuel pump, air is sucked into the tank through the filler neck. When that warm air hits the cool gasoline in the tank, the water vapor in it condenses and settles on tank walls and bottom.

Fuel tanks that have been sitting for years wind up containing a residue that will clog carburetors and cause engine valves to stick in their guides to the point where they have to be pounded out with a hammer and drift. Consequently, an old car that has been idle should have its gas tank refurbished before the car is put back on the road. Also, if you are doing a frame-up restoration, you will certainly want to clean and seal the gas tank.

Here's how its done.

SAFETY FIRST

Work outdoors if possible, keep a fire extinguisher nearby, and don't smoke or work anywhere near a water heater or clothes dryer. A pilot light or spark from these devices could easily cause an explosion. Also, before you begin taking out the tank, disconnect the ground (negative on most cars) lead to the battery to prevent a short and spark.

DRAIN THE FUEL

If your car has a drain plug on the fuel tank and you can get it open, draining the fuel is simple. Don't try to force the plug if it is rusted shut; you might ruin your tank. Use two gas cans and get a friend to help transfer the fuel. Be careful not to drop the drain plug into the waiting can. If the gas is fresh, put it in another car; if not, dispose of it according to local environmental laws.

If your car's tank doesn't have a drain plug (many newer ones don't), use an accordion-pleated, plastic siphon pump available from auto parts stores, or a hose with a squeeze bulb obtainable from a boat supply store to extricate the remaining fuel. Drain the gas into a container that is lower to the ground than the bottom of the tank. Don't be tempted to suck on the end of a hose to get the fuel started, though, because gasoline is quite toxic and irritating to your skin — you'll get a mouthful if you try it.

REMOVAL

Jack up the rear of the car, put it on sturdy jack stands, and block the front wheels. Disconnect the gas-gauge sending unit wire if possible and loosen the fuel-line coupling. Now loosen the steel straps or the bolts holding the tank in place. Let the tank down gently and get a friend to help pull it from under the car. Tanks are heavier than you might think and are unwieldy.

Place the tank on sawhorses outdoors and remove the gas-gauge sending unit. Look inside the hole for the sending unit to verify the condition of the tank lining. Do this outdoors using sunlight for illumination and for safety reasons, not a flashlight or your Bic lighter! If the lining of your tank is shiny, clean metal you're in luck. That is how it is supposed to look. But if it isn't, don't despair. Most old gas tanks can be cleaned and repaired.

If you live near a Redi-Strip or other automotive paint stripper you may want to have your tank stripped clean. It will come back looking like new and professional stripping can save you hours of work. Unfortunately, there aren't enough commercial automotive paint strippers to go around, and many have been forced out of business due to environmental concerns. An alternative is to take your tank to a radiator shop and have them hot tank it to clean it, then solder any holes. You can also clean the tank at home.

To clean your tank, duct tape the sending unit shut, then pour in a one-pound coffee can of old screws, nuts, and bolts. You can use sharp, pea gravel, but I don't recommend it because the stuff can give off silt and dust that could damage your engine. Shoot in a couple of quarts of water and slosh this mixture around to loosen scale and rust. Be sure to agitate the tank vigorously and   go over its inner surfaces completely with the nuts and bolts. Pour the mixture out and repeat the process until the water comes out clean.

Spots in this cutaway tank show how tanks rust from the inside due to condensation.

Holes can be soldered at a radiator-repair shop, but don't try it at home. Gasoline-permeated metal and fumes could cause an explosion.

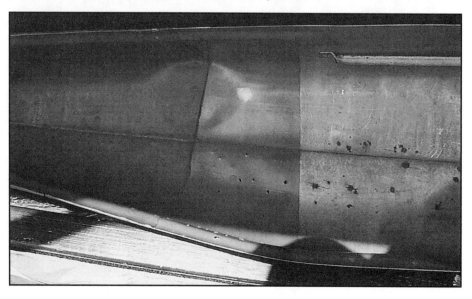

Tank repair consists of having it hot tanked, then fixing any big leaks, prepping it, and sealing it.

MAKING YOUR TANK LOOK ITS BEST

A big, rusty, dirty, unsightly gas tank will go a long way toward spoiling the appearance of your show-winning chassis. Once you have the thing out of the car, the job of making a gas tank look new is easy. Do a little research to determine how the tank was finished in the first place. On some older cars they were painted black, at least underneath. Most tanks had a nickel/tin coating or were bare steel.

As we said before, a commercial automotive paint stripper can do a good job of cleaning your tank and readying it for paint. Unfortunately, most of us have no commercial stripper nearby. In that case, here is a good way to clean up your tank's exterior. Duct tape the filler neck and the gas-gauge sending unit closed so as not to contaminate the interior.

Wash the tank down with a strong mixture of dishwasher detergent and water to remove dirt and grease. Now go over it with a good rust remover such as Oxisolv until you get down to clean, bare metal. Dry the tank thoroughly, then go over it with No. 80 grit open-coat sandpaper to remove any last bits of rust and to roughen the tank's surface so paint will adhere.

For a convincing galvanized look, shoot on Rustoleum clean-metal primer, then shoot on a coat of silver Rustoleum. Let it dry for a day or two, then shoot on another coat and blot it using coarse, artificial sponges while the paint is still wet. (Rustoleum is slow drying, so this is easily done.) I'm talking about the kind of synthetic sponges found in most people's kitchens. This method will give your tank that hot-dipped look. Let this second coat dry a day or two, then reinstall the tank.

For a zinc-coated, or bare-steel look, The Eastwood Company makes a product called Tank Tone that contains real zinc. It looks correct and helps stop corrosion. You'll need a couple of cans to do the job. Follow the directions on the can.

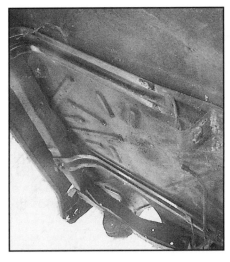

Once the tank is out, clean and detail the chassis where it attaches.

When you have your tank as clean as you can get it, check for leaks. With it still placed on sawhorses, fill it completely so that the water rises into the filler neck. Using a china marker or grease pencil, circle the leaks you find. Look for wet or rusty circular patches. Don't forget to check around the filler neck weld, too. Any holes can easily be soldered at a radiator shop.

Never try to solder leaks yourself. Even after sloshing it out with water, your tank can still contain explosive fumes. Inner surfaces will be permeated with gasoline that could be very dangerous. A

After the tank is cleaned, use a good chemical-prep solution to etch the metal and help it dry.

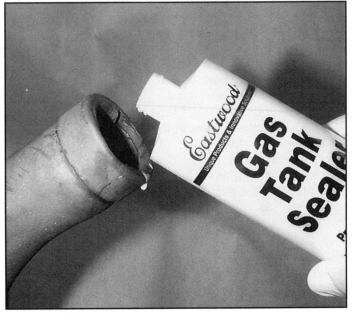

Pour in sealer and slosh it into every nook and cranny. A thin coat is better than a thick one. Let the tank dry, then coat it again to seal it thoroughly.

radiator shop will hot-tank your fuel tank, thus cleaning it further. They can then safely solder leaks.

If you only have a couple of tiny pin leaks you can seal them with a gas tank sealer and restorer kit. These are available from sources advertising in hobby publications. One popular system uses three different solutions. The first solution helps remove rust, the second displaces moisture, and the third seals the tank. Others have two solutions.

Whichever system you purchase, get a sealant that is alcohol resistant. Spiked fuel could wreak havoc with your fuel system. After cleaning the tank as thoroughly as possible, let it dry completely. Then, with the openings sealed, slosh sealer solution around so that every surface is coated. A thin coat is better than a thick one. Pour out the excess, let the tank dry for a day, then give it another coat. Let the tank cure for a week with orifices open before reinstalling it.

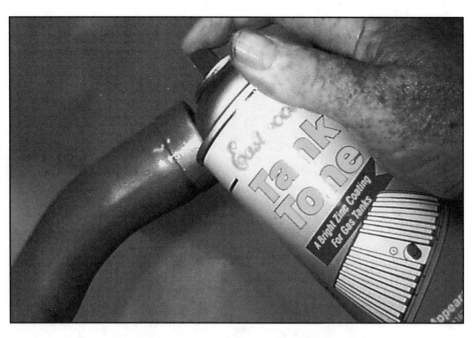

Eastwood's tank tone gives a gas tank that original zinc-plated look and holds up well.

RESTORING THE SENDING UNIT

If you are unsure whether the gas tank sending unit is in good order, connect it to a multi-meter and move the actuating lever through its range. The gauge should go up and down smoothly. If it does not, check your contacts and try again. If you still get no response, the rheostat inside probably is defective.

If the unit is working well, shoot it with a little paint in the outside surfaces, then clean the electrical contacts. Let the sending unit's cork dry for several hours, then dip it in shellac and let it dry again before installing the unit in the tank.

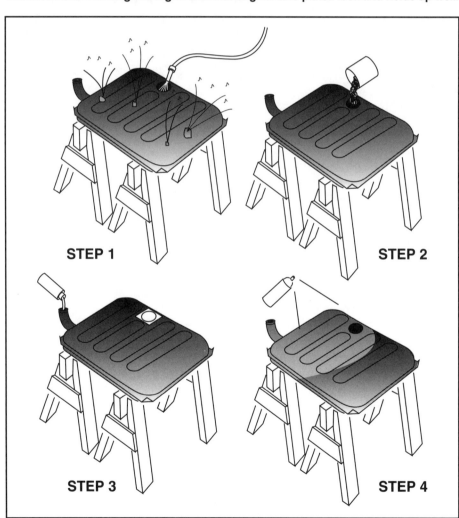

STEP 1

STEP 2

STEP 3

STEP 4

Fill with water and check for leaks. Use a grease pencil to circle them, then have a radiator shop solder any big ones. 2) Pour in a bucket of bolts and a couple of quarts of water and slosh them around thoroughly to dislodge rust. 3) Let the tank dry thoroughly, then slosh tank prep through it to dry it and prepare it for sealant. Pour in sealant and slosh it thoroughly. Do this several times to insure a good seal. 4) Paint your tank according to original specs. Some were matte black, others were galvanized, and others were zinc coated or bare steel.

S·A DESIGN

Tires

Some years ago, a young man in my neighborhood decided to make a dune buggy out of his Volkswagen Bug. Never mind that we live hundreds of miles from any dunes, he was mostly after a certain look. He added a special fiberglass engine cover, a roll bar, ran an intake duct and air filter up to the top of the car, and installed a stinger exhaust that stuck straight up like a chrome-plated skunk tail. He then mounted some gigantic tires on the back that looked as if they would be more at home on a military deuce-and-a-half than on a VW Beetle.

This setup lasted him about two weeks. You see, those big, fat back tires and those wide wheels put so much stress on the axle bearings that they soon failed. And of course the Bug's velocity joints and half shafts were never the same after that, either. Also, the car wasn't too brisk getting away from a traffic light with those big shoes on it because they had

the same effect on his car as adding taller gears.

I can't judge the lad too harshly, though. Who among us hasn't put a set of fat, fancy, aftermarket tires on a car, mostly for cosmetic reasons? Most of us have done it, blissfully unaware that doing so sometimes adds up to big — and occasionally dangerous — problems. Tires are the most critical component in both your car's drive line and suspension system. Automotive engineers have long been aware of this and have designed their products accordingly over the years.

Every car produced in any quantity in the last 60 years was designed to have tires of a specific diameter, width, rubber compound, and load-carrying capacity. Steering geometry, handling, ride, gas mileage, and chassis function all depend heavily on having the correct types of tires on your car. To do otherwise would be dangerous. Two examples of what I'm talking about took place in 1964 at

the Indianapolis 500.

That year the Mickey Thompson Special — aptly nicknamed the Skate — came to the track shod with 13-in. rims and tires. These did not comply with existing track regulations, so 15-in. rims and tires were substituted at the last minute. The result was a car that handled so badly the intended driver, Graham Hill, refused to drive it. Instead, a young hot-shoe named Dave McDonald put the car in the field. Sadly, he spun on the second lap of the race and collided with veteran Eddie Sachs who was just coming out of the fourth turn. The result was one of the most horrific crashes in Indy history. It killed both drivers, critically injured another, and wrecked seven cars.

When the race was restarted, Jimmy Clark led easily until a disintegrating tire wrecked his suspension and put him out of the race. A.J. Foyt went on to win in an old, front-engined roadster that wasn't competitive.

That's because he didn't have any tire problems. Anyone who follows any kind of racing knows that tires are just as critical to a driver's success today as they were in '64. Tires are critical to your classic, too.

Whether your car was made 10, 20, or 60 years ago, it was designed to accommodate a particular kind of tire. But, you might say, tires have been improved immensely over the last few years. This is so, but as often as not, changing a classic to modern tires has adverse results if you aren't careful. Here are examples of what I'm talking about.

When I bought my '57 Chev 210 a few years ago it had smaller diameter, modern, steel-belted radial tires. They didn't look good on the car, but that was the least of my worries. They were also noisy. The car drummed as it went down the road. The handling was twitchy and the speedometer didn't read right because the tires were the wrong diameter. And they were dangerous. A full-size '57 Chev is no lightweight, and the load-carrying capacity of the new radials wasn't even close to adequate for the job they were required to do.

The previous owner thought the radials would make the car handle better, but the opposite turned out

to be true. Such 1950s-era sedans weren't designed to handle well. They were designed to be comfortable on all kinds of roads. Bumps were to be discretely implied, not jarring. If you don't like the handling of such a car, you'll need to make some fairly extensive modifications to improve things. You'd be smarter to opt for a more nimble machine rather than try to outguess the engineers who designed your land yacht.

And then there are the people who install much wider tires. A little wider tire can be a good thing sometimes, but real wide is a real problem. Such tires might improve a car's handling in some circumstances, but they will make it harder to steer, noisier, and more subject to aquaplaning in wet weather. Also, fat tires can stress chassis components that were not designed for them.

Whether you car's tires are too big, too small, too fat, too skinny, too soft, or too hard, it all adds up to the same thing. Your vintage vehicle will not ride and feel the way it was designed to and you may be running unnecessary risks in the bargain. I don't mean that you have to scout the country to find 40-year-old nylon-ply tires if that is what the car came with. There are a couple of companies that can provide you with updated

equivalents that are in fact superior to the originals and are made specifically to replace them. If you are having trouble locating correct tires for your car, try these sources:

Universal Tire Co., Inc.
987 Stone Battery Rd.
Lancaster, PA 17601
Phone (800) 233-3827

Coker Tire Co.
1317 Chestnut St.
Chattanooga, TN 37402
Phone (800)251-6336
Fax (615) 756-5607

DO I NEED NEW TIRES?

How do you know if your classic needs new tires? One way to tell if a tire is worn out is to insert a penny into the tread with the top of Lincoln's head toward the casing. If the tread does not come up at least to Honest Abe's scalp, you definitely need new tires. Bald tires will make your car very dangerous in wet situations. Also, such tires will be more prone to puncture and will cause a harsher ride, too.

Another sure indication that you need new tires is when you see a bulge on the sidewall or the tread. This means that there is a breach in the structural integrity of the

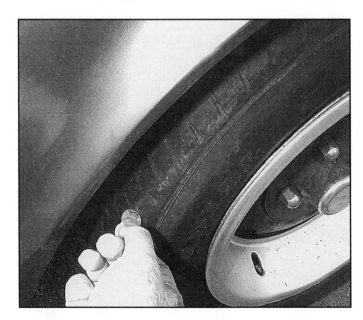

If the tread on your tires doesn't come up to Abe Lincoln's scalp on a penny, it's time for new tires.

This tiny tire is an accident waiting to happen. Not only is it not the right diameter or width, making this old truck a handful to drive, but its load-carrying capacity is not up to the job of supporting the vehicle.

Fat tires and offset wheels add up to problems that might require a fat wallet to fix. They cause stress to axle bearings and make for harder steering and unnecessary wear on components.

Differentials rarely give trouble, but with enough neglect and abuse, they will fail. First, the owner of this older work truck put tires of two different sizes on the rear axle, causing the differential to work against itself. As a result, the small, spider gears in the center wore out, along with their bearings. The owner also failed to change the lubricant at the proper intervals, so the ring and pinion gears went south. This kind of damage need not happen if basic procedures are followed. Never run tires of two sizes on the rear of your car, and keep that rear end topped up with fluid.

casing, such as torn cords or separating plies. There is no way to fix such a tire. Putting in a tube if the tire is tubeless may keep the air from leaking out, but it won't repair the structural damage.

Cuts through the casing, whether they are in the sidewall or the tread, also mean that the tire should be replaced. Sometimes, white sidewalls will check, crack, or come away from the casing. That's because white rubber is naturally more biodegradable than black, so it tends to deteriorate first. Such blemishes give your classic an unpleasant appearance, but they don't usually mean serious trouble.

Those are the more obvious things. Some less obvious, but not compelling, tire problems can also spell trouble. On cars that have been idle for years, the tires — though they may have all of the original tread — will become hard and stiff. Such tires are dangerously prone to failure; even if they weren't, you will want to replace them because they will make your car ride badly. Tires are supposed to flex every time you go over a bump to absorb small irregularities in the road. If your tires are stiff and hard, they will transfer everything to the car's suspension, steering, and ultimately, to you.

TREAD TELLS THE TALE

A number of problems show up in the wear patterns of your tire treads sooner or later. Most of them are simple and easily remedied. Probably the most easily corrected problem is underinflation. When you drive on tires that are underinflated, their sidewalls are wrenched and flexed in ways that will soon destroy the structural integrity. Also, because of added friction with the road surface, heat builds up. Sooner or later, tires that are underinflated will wear on their outer edges, leaving the center tread comparatively untouched.

Overinflation will make your car ride badly and can make its handling rather sensitive. Weekend

This tire is worn on the outside due to excessive negative camber, probably as a result of collision with a curb.

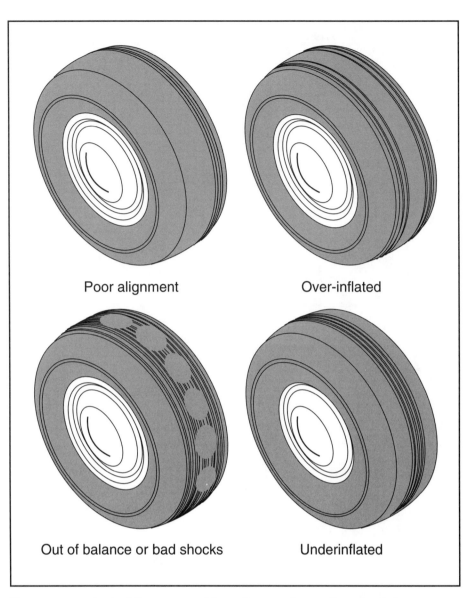

Poor alignment

Over-inflated

Out of balance or bad shocks

Underinflated

Here are some typical tire wear problems than can be easily remedied.

racers sometimes slightly overinflate their tires to make their cars more responsive and a little faster, thanks to the decreased friction with the road. But overinflation comes at a price. Their tires will wear in the middle, leaving the outer edges of the treads comparatively untouched. These hay-bale racers also sometimes dial in a fair amount of positive camber on the front wheels to make the car more stable, but this too makes short work of good tires.

A different set of problems that show up as odd wear patterns in tire treads has to do with wheel alignment. Excessive positive camber can make tires wear on the inside margins of treads. Too much negative camber can cause tires to wear only on the outside edges of the treads. Toe-in or toe-out problems (toe-in is the automotive equivalent of being pigeon toed) can cause a rapid scrubbing of tread off tires. Back axles that are misaligned because they have been knocked cockeyed can cause wear, too. This problem can

result from the axle being loose in its mounts, which is easy to fix, or because a rear frame horn has been bent as a result of a collision, which is not so easy to fix.

Another problem that can effect front and rear tires is wheel balance. Tires, wheels, and even brake drums are usually heavier on one side than the other. When you consider that a tire and wheel can easily weigh as much as 40 pounds on the average older, full-size American car, that much weight spinning rapidly in an out-of-balance condition will start bouncing like a rubber ball at speed. Your car's suspension will absorb most of the vibration, but you will feel some of it telegraphing through the steering system. If your tires are out of balance, they

will wear in a cupped, or scooped-out pattern.

Another situation that can be very harmful to your car — even though it won't usually do damage to your tires — is to run different tire sizes, especially on the rear axle. When you do, the differential has to work against itself and will wear out quickly. Different size tires, even different tread patterns and depths on the same car, can affect handling. Don't rely on the numbers stamped on the sidewalls to tell you that your tires are all the same size if they came from different manufacturers or are of different ages.

One way to check tire circumference is to use a tailor's tape measure. Another way is to make a mark on the side of the tire and a corresponding mark on the floor,

Michelin Pilot XGT V4

Michelin Pilot HX MXM

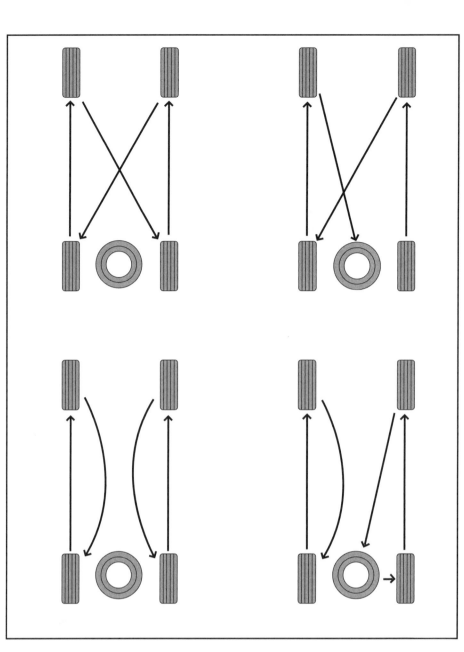

Rotate your tires regularly. Here are some typical rotation diagrams. Check with your tire dealer as to which is appropriate to your chassis. Don't switch sides with radials.

BF Goodrich Comp T/A ZR SSS

BF Goodrich Comp T/A ZR

BF Goodrich G-Force T/A R1

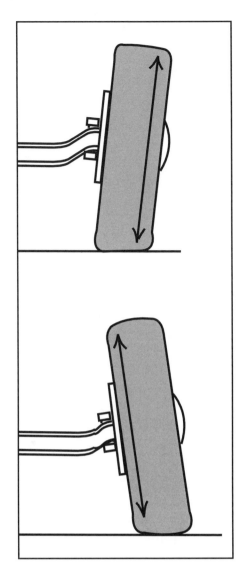

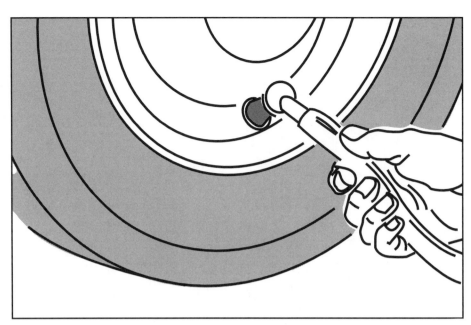

Make sure your tires are inflated to the correct pressure at least once a week or every time you take your classic out for a drive if you only drive it occasionally.

Top illustration shows what happens when you have too much negative camber. Bottom shows too much positive camber. Either will wear out tires in a hurry.

then have a friend drive your car forward until the mark comes around to the bottom again and then measure along the pavement. Circumference can be affected by speed, too. A soft, flexible tire will increase in diameter from centrifugal force more than a stiff, hard tire, so different makes of tires may not behave the same way at freeway speeds.

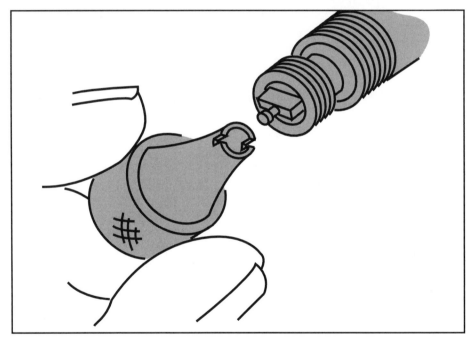

Make sure valves are tight in stems so you don't develop a slow leak.

MAINTENANCE PREVENTS PROBLEMS

Here are some simple tips for making your tires last longer.

Keep them inflated to the manufacturer's specifications. Only check them when they are cold, because pressure builds with the heat of rolling friction. If you check your tires after a stint of highway driving, the pressure will appear too high.

Have your car's tires balanced every time you purchase new ones. On old, softly sprung cars this is especially critical, because tires will bounce themselves to bits at high speeds if they are out of balance.

Rotate your tires at the interval specified by the manufacturer. Take a tip from the racers and don't switch sides when rotating radials. Doing so will cause the steel belts to flex, first one way then the other, resulting in metal fatigue and possible failure.

Have your front end aligned every time you install new tires. Your car will handle better and your tires will last longer. If your car has four-wheel independent suspension, have the back wheels aligned, as well.

Engine & Chassis DETAILING
Putting It Together

Putting a car together after it has been apart is a little trickier than most people realize. The driveline must line up, the front suspension and steering must be right, and all those body panels need to align correctly so they look right and open and close without ruining the paint. How many cars have you seen where the hood corners are crumpled because the hood was installed too far back? Then there is the uncomfortable feeling you get when a car's body is just a little out of plumb. It spoils the appearance entirely. Fortunately, there are a few techniques you can use to keep this from happening to your classic.

For instance, there is a little trick I used years ago when I worked assembling Falcons and Fairlanes in a Ford plant. My job was to install the passenger-side front fender. The door was already in place when the car got to me. Then I only had a minute to pick up my fender, position it, bolt it into place from the top, then hold the

kick panel in place while a co-worker in a pit bolted the fender into place at the bottom.

Here's the trick: I would throw a piece of carpeting on the forward edge of the door, jam the fender against it — which would give me the proper 3/16-in. clearance — then line up the sheet metal fender apron with an awl and bolt the assembly together. I still use carpet pieces the same way to help protect paint and to establish clearances between doors, decks, lids, and fenders.

Fenders and hoods must fit with a consistent gap all around and they must open easily without damage. Ditto for doors and deck lids. The carpet trick is great for that. Obviously, bumpers need to line up correctly, too. And doors and deck lids shouldn't stick out at the top or bottom or at the corners.

So how do you make sure such things don't happen to you? There is no mystery to it, but you need to take your time and you need to measure. The difficulty of putting a

car back together, of course, is directly proportional to the amount of patience and effort you put into taking it apart. If you ripped into the job in a big hurry and simply threw all the fasteners in a coffee can, the job will be tricky.

On the other hand, if you took your time, took photos, scribed around door hinges, hood hinges, and trunk hinges so you could align things as they were originally when putting the car back together; and if you saved and labeled all the shims and washers you removed, the job will be an easy one.

PROTECT THE PAINT

After all that body work, priming, painting, and color sanding, you won't want to nick, scratch, or damage your finish work any more than necessary. Fact is, you are bound to do a little damage just bolting things together. It can't be helped. Later, we'll tell you how to fix these minor assembly nicks so they disappear. For the time being, though, be as careful as you can, but don't fret unnecessarily.

Most likely, by now your car has been apart for some time. Don't get impatient at this point and try to hurry things. Let the paint cure and harden for a couple of weeks before reassembling the car. You don't want to pull fresh paint off with the protective masking tape we are going to use.

In the meantime, gather all the old blankets, bubble wrap, and Styrofoam chunks you can find. You will also need the aforementioned masking tape and the 6 x 6-in. squares of short-nap carpeting. (Pick these up at a carpet outlet.) Schedule a friend or spouse to help with big pieces such as hoods, deck lids, and doors. You won't be able to hold these items in place yourself while installing the fasteners.

Protect the edges of openings for bumpers and bright work with masking tape to prevent scratching the paint before assembly. Do this even if rubber grommets will cover the nicked edges as in the case of a bumper bracket, because any place you leave bare metal exposed will be an entry point for rust. Grommets can't

keep moisture out completely.

I like to use blocks of Styrofoam to prevent nicks on the rear corners of hoods and on the corners of doors. Simply cut a block of foam with a utility knife, slit it, then tape it in place until you are ready to install the item. Use carpet squares between such places as the forward edges of doors and the rear edges of fenders to prevent damage and to help maintain the correct gap.

DOORS

Get a friend to help with door installation. There is no way you can do it properly by yourself. You run a big risk of damaging the door and its jamb if you try. Begin by placing a thick blanket on the floor so you can rest the door on it without chipping the paint. Now, if the door is light enough for a friend to hold in position so its hinges line up with the body, bolt it loosely into place. If the door is heavy, use jack stands and wooden shims covered by foam blocks to support the door while your friend holds it in alignment. If you scribed around the hinges to establish location before removing the doors, just jig-

gle the door until the hinge fits into the scribed lines and bolt it into place.

If you neglected to scribe the locations where the door hinges bolt in, you will have to play with the thing for a while until you get it completely aligned. The door must not sag at the rear, must not be too far forward or back, and must not stick out at the top or bottom. Use scraps of carpet to protect the paint while you are doing your fitting. Work slowly, close and open the door slowly, and if it starts to bind anywhere, stop immediately to determine where it is misaligned. This is a painstaking but

On cars made in the '30s and '40s, there often were two rods to support and adjust the radiator and grille shell, as on the author's 1936 Packard touring sedan. If you didn't twiddle with the adjustments of these when you took the car apart, they should be fairly close when you put the car back together.

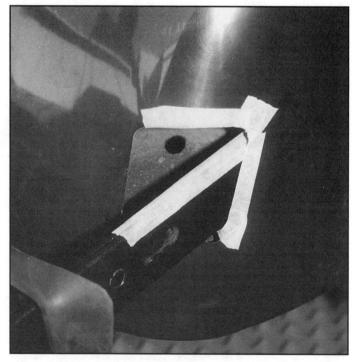

Use masking tape to protect edges of sheet metal during reassembly. Even little nicks that will be hidden by grommets will attract moisture and invite rust.

Measure along each side of the grille shell during reassembly to make sure the edges are equidistant from the cowl on both sides.

The door on this '59 Chev is too far back, so it will be hard to close and the paint on the rear edge will chip. Loosen the hinges and move it forward slightly.

necessary process.

If the door doesn't line up right, it can spring open on the road while cornering, or it may bind and chip the paint. Don't try to move the striker plate in the door jamb to meet a misaligned door. When the door closes with a reassuring "chunk" and meets its striker place cleanly, you are most of the way there. Then all you have to do is make sure it lays flush with the rest of the body when closed and that the gap all the way around the door is consistent.

FENDERS AND FENDER APRONS

On more modern cars, the rear quarter panels act as fenders. On earlier cars with bolt-on fenders, there is no particular problem with getting rear fenders to fit. Tape edges, bolt the fender loosely in place using the correct large-fender washers, then when you have the fender located visually, remove the tape and tighten everything evenly. Don't over-tighten and crack the paint.

Front fenders and sheet metal are a little trickier. The inner fender aprons and radiator support braces are installed first and left a little loose. Now install the fenders, using the proper welt or weather stripping between each fender and its apron. Use carpet squares to keep the fenders from bimping the doors and again, bolt the fender loosely into place.

Have your helper hold one end of a piece of string along the length of the car while you hold the other. Hold the string straight, near the side of the car, on one side and then the other, to check for misalignment. Front fenders can easily be tweaked to the left or right, causing the whole front end to look as if the car had been hit. Also, one fender can be off from its vertical axis at the front, causing the other to follow, with the result that the front end of the car will look cockeyed.

If you suspect this type of misalignment, have your helper hold a plumb bob in front of each headlight to verify alignment. When the fenders are as they should be, tighten all the bolts. Install the grille and headlights and check alignment again. Later, you will need to aim the headlights according to the instructions in your service manual.

HOOD AND TRUNK LIDS

Once again, if you scribed around the hinges and saved all the shims, noting their locations before removing the hood and trunk lid, the job of alignment will be pretty straightforward. If you didn't do these things at the outset, you will need to be especially careful with the hood to prevent binding and chipping.

For the hood as well as the deck lid, put blankets over the fenders, place Styrofoam blocks on the corners of the hood, then snug up the hood or deck lid on its hinges. Now remove the blankets and foam blocks and slowly lower the hood to see if it binds or closes smoothly. Don't force anything. If you meet resistance, stop and readjust the alignment to eliminate it. When the hood and deck lid close smoothly and meet the latches squarely, tighten their attaching bolts fully.

On earlier cars, use the rods that go from the firewall to the radiator frame to align the grille, hood, and fender assembly (front clip). Again, the radiator and grille must be upright, or vertical, not tipped back or leaning forward in their cradle. If you didn't change the dimensions of the rods by turning their adjusting nuts, you should be able to bolt the front clip together loosely, then use the rods to fine tune the alignment. When everything is squared up, tighten all the bolts evenly, a little at a time.

TOUCH UP

As we said at the beginning, you will make a few nicks and scratches when putting your car back together. But that's not much of a problem because minor scratches are easy to fix. With a small, soft,

Now the door sticks too far out and hangs too low. Further tinkering with hinges should fix it.

The door on the other side of our Chevy is fine at the bottom, but too far in at the top. To fix it, the upper hinge will need to be moved slightly or shimmed.

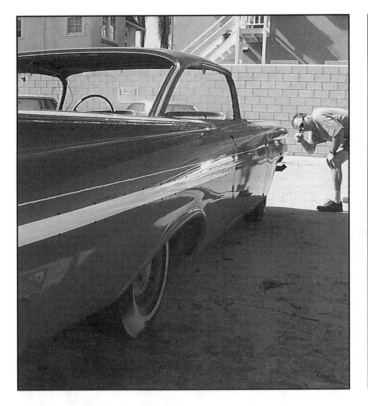

String can make a nice straight datum line along which you can sight and look for irregularities. Be sure to check both sides and compare.

Measure from the ground to the headlights to make sure body work is level on both corners at the front end. If it isn't, loosen fasteners and carefully readjust.

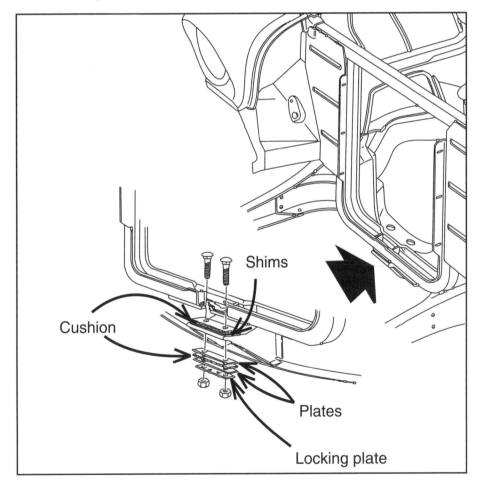

If you didn't save the shims, pads, and hardware when you took the front clip off your car, you will find aligning the clip a tricky proposition. Belt moldings must be straight and parallel and fenders must stand up straight when viewed from the front.

camel's hair brush, dab — don't brush — drops of leftover paint into the scratch, letting it dry between dabs. The Eastwood Company makes a paint pen and touch-up kit that is ideal for this job. Apply several coats until the scratch or nick stands above the surrounding paint.

Let this dry for a couple of weeks, then, using a hard rubber sanding block or the one in your Eastwood kit made especially for this job, and No. 1000 microfine grit, wet sandpaper and water, sand the surface of your touched-up spot down to the surrounding paint. Go over this with No. 2000 grit, then rub it out and polish it to match the rest of the finish. That's all there is to it. Now your chariot should be a vision of loveliness and straight as an arrow. Take photos, because it will never be this perfect again.

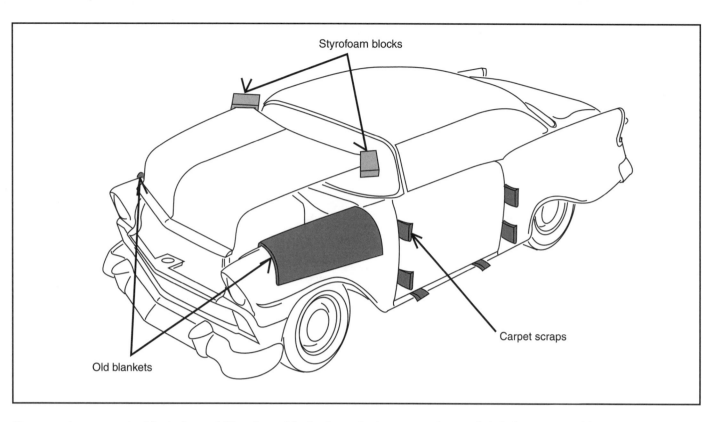

Styrofoam blocks

Carpet scraps

Old blankets

Use carpet scrap pads, blankets, and Styrofoam blocks to protect your precious paint during reassembly.

Do let your paint cure for at least two weeks before assembly.

Do check panel alignment carefully.

Do use protective coverings to prevent chipped paint.

Do work slowly and carefully.

Do attach things loosely until all fasteners are installed, then tighten evenly.

Don't over-tighten fasteners.

Don't move door striker plates to accommodate misaligned doors.

Don't try to position hoods and doors by yourself.

Don't set parts on hard floors with no protection under them while working.

Don't make big adjustments. Move things a little at a time until they line up correctly.

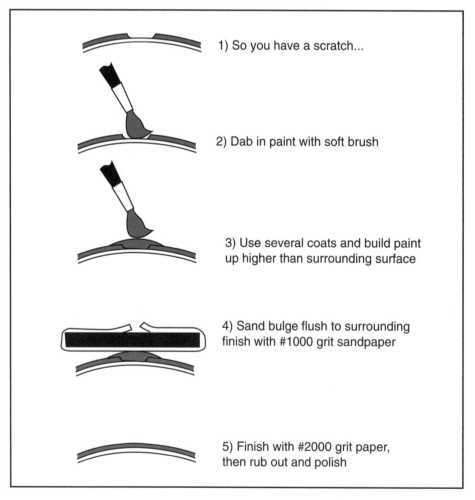

1) So you have a scratch...

2) Dab in paint with soft brush

3) Use several coats and build paint up higher than surrounding surface

4) Sand bulge flush to surrounding finish with #1000 grit sandpaper

5) Finish with #2000 grit paper, then rub out and polish

Build paint up in dabs until it stands a little above the surrounding surface. Let it cure, then sand with No. 1000 grit microfine sandpaper. Go over with No. 2000 grit, then rub and polish.

NOTES:

NOTES:

NOTES: